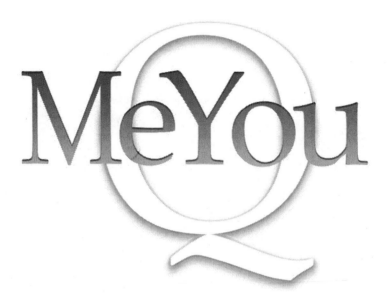

Life-Changing Protocols

for People Leaders

Printed by CreateSpace, Charleston, SC

Available from Amazon.com and other retail outlets

ISBN: 978-1-7751433-0-7

Content Editor: Craig Dyer
(https://www.linkedin.com/in/craig-dyer-655b592)

Copy Editor: Shauna Stevenson
(https:www.linkedin.com/in/shauna-stevenson-1362408b)

Cover Design: Ann Poten

The advice in this book is not a substitute for legal advice for specific situations. Names used do not reflect the characteristics of an actual person.

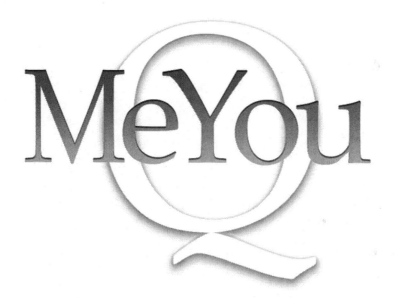

Table of Contents

Forward by the Author

OVER THE LAST 18 YEARS, I have had the privilege of working with many college and industry students, preparing them for careers in the business world. Over the years, many students have told me that they learned a lot in my human resources and supervision courses, and that everyone could benefit from taking them. This got me thinking that it would be great to be able to offer courses to a wider audience. With this in mind, I began developing a program to provide comprehensive training for supervisors, through my business, *TREE for Supervisors.*

I have always believed that people need to be treated better in the workplace, so I wanted to create a tool with the potential to have a major impact on the work environment, but one that could also be applied by individuals to other areas of their lives. In its conceptual stage, this system seemed a lot like Daniel Goleman's Emotional Intelligence (EQ), which measures how well a person can recognize his or her emotions, as well as those of others, and manage or adjust them to preserve relationships and achieve their goals. As the concept evolved, however, it became clear that the program I envisioned involved a much more holistic approach; encompassing mind, body, and spirit in addition to emotions, and as such it should have its own "Q" designation, which led to the term "*MeYouQ*."

MeYouQ involves connecting to and managing all of the traits that make up a person. In order to have genuine connections with others, however, we must first connect within ourselves. *MeYouQ* is about recognizing, understanding, embracing, and managing all of our own characteristics, including our emotions, so that we can behave appropriately in a variety of situations while appreciating and respecting the many traits of other people. It is only when we achieve this awareness that we can begin to value ourselves and others, and build productive working relationships.

The *MeYouQ* process will help supervisors develop their own leadership style, control their behavior to gain the respect of others, be less judgmental and more accepting of all employees, provide equal attention and opportunity to everyone, have meaningful exchanges, and strive to help employees feel satisfied and be engaged at work. It is a tool for relating to people and forming the kinds of relationships needed to encourage staff to work hard for their organization. By modeling the *MeYouQ* process, supervisors can truly connect with employees, and can teach them to use the process as well.

MeYouQ is not just for supervisors; it can be used by anyone, in any situation, to help people transform their lives and their relationships. The *MeYouQ* process will help individuals find inner peace, see their own purpose in life, be more accepting of others, have better interpersonal relationships, and be able to work through feelings of conflict successfully, in a positive way.

The "Me" in *MeYouQ* refers to self-acceptance. This is an integral part of the process, which will guide you to explore what makes you who you are and help you to realize that this is who you are supposed to be. As you learn to value and accept yourself, you may also see that you need to adjust your behavior to achieve your goals in life. You work from recognizing your different traits to understanding the impact of your traits on your behavior to managing your behavior, so it is appropriate for the situation. *MeYouQ* will help you reach your full potential by teaching you to make conscious choices and to embrace your purpose on this earth. When you are experiencing an internal struggle, you can call on *MeYouQ* to remind you to accept yourself as you are.

The "You" in *MeYouQ* will show you how to accept and value the people in both your personal and professional lives. You will learn to turn off negative reactions to the behaviors of others and see them as unique individuals with a variety of traits, just as you are a unique individual with a variety of traits. As you become less judgmental, you will recognize that each person behaves a certain way because of his or her characteristics and has his or her own special contribution to make. When the actions of others cause you stress, you can call on *MeYouQ* to remind you to accept others and allow them to be who they are.

Finally, the "Q" in *MeYouQ* refers to your capacity to combine the ability to manage yourself with the ability to accept differences in others, while developing good working relationships with people in all areas of your life. The need to be at peace with yourself and the people around you is crucial to living your purpose with confidence. You will be able to communicate in a way that will help each person get what they need out of the relationship while being more effective and fulfilled in your life. An open mind and the desire to have a better life are all that are required.

Introduction to *MeYouQ*

What kind of life-changing experience are you seeking?

IT'S FUNNY HOW THOSE MUST-DO, bucket list sorts of things end up being disappointing. You are looking for some great life-changing experience and it doesn't happen. It can be this way with your personal or professional life; most of us have a list of things we want to achieve in each of these areas. You may be just starting out in your career, or perhaps you are a little more experienced. You may have had many personal life experiences, or maybe only a few. Some things have been disappointing, but some things have impacted your life greatly. All kinds of experiences change our lives; what kind of change are you looking for in your life right now, and what will lead to that change?

MeYouQ: *Life-Changing Protocols for People Leaders* aims to bring you the tools you need to change your life and the lives of the people you work with. If you are looking for more peace in your life and better results from your team, you have picked up the right book. Once you complete your *MeYouQ* journey, you will have better control over your thoughts and behaviors, and you will be more in tune with the thoughts and behaviors of those around you. This journey culminates with your ability to build better relationships and supervise people for good

1

psychological health and safety. While this book is geared towards people leaders, the *MeYouQ* process can be used in both personal and professional situations.

Do you have conflict at work? Is it conflict over resources and methods, or because people can't get along? In a world where teamwork is becoming increasingly important, there is no time for personality conflicts in business. You cannot simply avoid the people you work with; you need to find a way to successfully work together.

What does it mean to "successfully work together"? A successful work relationship is one in which people are showing respect for each other's ideas; sharing information; and making decisions, solving problems, and innovating together. This is not going to be possible if you cannot stand the sight of each other or resolve your differences.

MeYouQ helps you to develop an appreciation for others by first appreciating yourself. It asks you to break down your beliefs about how other people should act, so you can accept them for who they are. By breaking down these intra- and interpersonal barriers, you are then able to work on building productive relationships. Remember that any real change must come from within. *MeYouQ* will teach you how to take responsibility for your thoughts and behaviors and show you how to use these new insights to build stronger connections with others.

Does work stress you out? Do the people at work constantly annoy you? A report by Graham Winfrey[1] published by Inc.com stated administrators in the United States spend an average of 2.5 hours per week dealing with conflict, at a cost of $359 billion. Just think of all the time and money your organization can save if employees and their bosses can achieve better interpersonal relations! As you develop *MeYouQ*, you will find that other people bother you less, and you are better able to view them in a positive light.

Is your goal to work your way up and become a manager? Many people are deterred from taking on management positions because of the extra stress involved. Does the thought of dealing with difficult employees and all of those different personalities prevent you from taking on a leadership role, even though you really want to get ahead? Do you want to develop the skills needed to be a people leader?

MeYouQ is a system that can be learned, and using these skills will bring more peace to all aspects of your life. *MeYouQ* will help you become the type of person people want to be around and follow. It will teach you how to bring out the best in others— qualities that are already there but you will now be able to recognize and appreciate.

Does your department experience high turnover? Are you disciplining and terminating people all too regularly? Are

---

[1] https://www.inc.com/graham-winfrey/the-shocking-cost-of-workplace-conflicts.html

employees frequently filing grievances? Is there a lot of time wasted with gossip and complaining? Each of these events has a monetary cost to the organization and a psychological impact to you and your employees, whether or not they are directly involved. As you build better relationships with the people you work with using the **MeYouQ** protocols, you will notice a decrease in the incidence of these events. You will be able to have the kinds of conversations with employees that are necessary in order for them to meet your standards. You will be able to tune into each person's traits and behaviors, allowing you to relate to them on a different level. You will gain more cooperation and be able to provide an engaging, supportive environment for your staff.

These are just a few situations where **MeYouQ** can change your life. The **MeYouQ** process begins with examining your own behavior and recognizing that your behavior is a product of your personal characteristics. Once you tune into your "self" and are mindful of choosing appropriate behavior, you are able to turn your attention towards understanding the behavior of those around you. When interacting with others, you will keep an open mind about their intentions and abilities, while working to see each individual as having his or her own unique strengths. Finally, when you identify a person's strengths and traits, you are better able to treat him as he would like to be treated, set him up for success in his area of expertise, and build a relationship with him. *(Note: instead of seeing "he" or "she" and "him" or "her" throughout the book, either the masculine or feminine version will be used. Please note that all situations apply to both genders).*

4

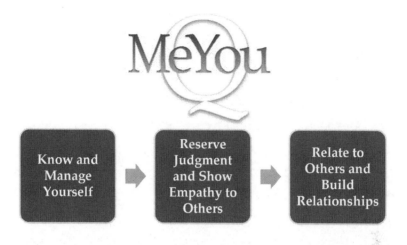

The first three parts of this book are designed to show you how to build your skills in **MeYouQ**. This life-changing process begins with self-awareness and self-management. In Part 1, you will learn how to appreciate yourself as a multifaceted individual; recognizing that you do what you do because of your unique traits. By becoming more aware of your actions, you will consciously choose them; this will help you not only to build better relationships with others, but also to lead a more purposeful, meaningful life.

In Part 2, you will work on understanding why others behave the way they do. As you learn to refrain from judging people or allowing their behaviors to bother you, you will become better able to accept them and look past their differences. You will be more at peace around others when you accept them as individuals, without expectations or preconceptions about how they should behave.

The *MeYouQ* process wraps up in Part 3, where you will use this newfound appreciation for others to build better working relationships at your job and in your personal life. You will take a holistic perspective when viewing others and focus on what you can do to connect with them. You'll be able to see past your differences and find common ground on which to move forward. Together, you negotiate how the relationship will function, and you check in regularly to make sure it is working. This allows people leaders to get results from employees, while supporting them holistically.

In Part 4 of the book, you will learn supervisory skills and management development theory, with special attention being put on supervising for good psychological health and safety in the workplace. You need to develop your *MeYouQ* if you are going to be the type of people leader who can provide or contribute to a psychologically healthy workplace and answer the "What's In It For Me (WIIFM)?" question for employees. When your employees feel you care about and understand them, they will work harder for you and be able to have more open conversations with you about their needs at work. Even if you are not a people leader, these protocols will provide many ideas for improving your own psychological well-being at work. In addition, you will be prepared for a future opportunity as a team leader or supervisor. Regardless of your position, you may also be able to influence the development of *MeYouQ* in others.

Congratulations on taking this step forward in your personal growth. Take your time working through the book and use the website, www.meyouqbook.com, password: pY23tD4c26, for additional support along the way. Now, get your pen or pencil ready, as you will be put to work. Turn the page as you set the intention to grow your *MeYouQ* and have the life-changing experience for which you have been searching!

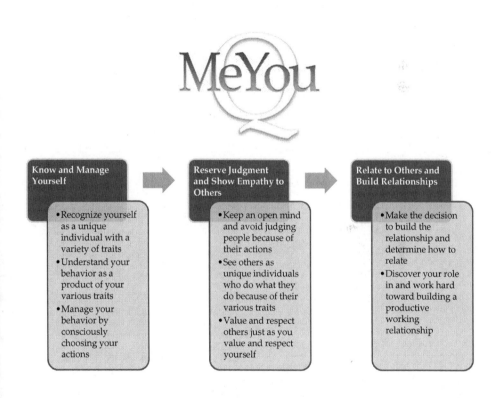

Know and Manage Yourself

- Recognize yourself as a unique individual with a variety of traits
- Understand your behavior as a product of your various traits
- Manage your behavior by consciously choosing your actions

Reserve Judgment and Show Empathy to Others

- Keep an open mind and avoid judging people because of their actions
- See others as unique individuals who do what they do because of their various traits
- Value and respect others just as you value and respect yourself

Relate to Others and Build Relationships

- Make the decision to build the relationship and determine how to relate
- Discover your role in and work hard toward building a productive working relationship

MeYouQ Self-Assessment

BEFORE BEGINNING YOUR *MeYouQ* journey, complete the following pre-test. This will help you see what you are going to learn and give you a sense of how well you are already doing in each area. If you completely agree with the statement, put a plus sign; if you disagree or don't know, put a minus.

Behavior	+ or -
1. I think about and consciously choose my behavior	
2. I often put the needs of others ahead of my own	
3. I am at peace with who I am; I accept myself	
4. I follow up and do what I say I will do	
5. I ensure my relationships are not one-sided	
6. I generally find people enjoyable and interesting	
7. I would say that, in general, people like me	
8. I often feel very positive and optimistic	
9. People often say nice things about me	
10. I am easily able to see others' points of view	
11. I am open to new ideas and methods	
12. I play and work well with others	
13. I find it easy to show an interest in others	
14. I monitor my behavior and act appropriately	
15. I don't hold grudges when someone has harmed me	
16. I am respectful when addressing difficult issues	
17. I love the people in my life unconditionally	
18. It is ok if people have standards different from mine	
19. I believe each person has a unique gift to share	
20. People understand me the first time I say something	
21. I treat others the way they want to be treated	
22. I value people who are different/think differently	
23. I find it easy to get to know people on a personal level	
24. I believe I am here on earth for a reason	

25. I have many good relationships, personal and work	
Total + Signs	

Did you add up your plus signs? A total of 20 or more would indicate you are well on your way to having high *MeYouQ*. A score between 15 and 19 is average with room for improvement. A total of 14 or less means you can benefit greatly from the exercises in this book. Whatever your score, use it as a baseline for now. You will have the opportunity to reassess at the end of Part 3, when the *MeYouQ*–building portions are completed.

Consider that real change takes time and reflection. Enjoy the process of self-reflection and growth. Begin now with Part 1: Know and Manage Yourself.

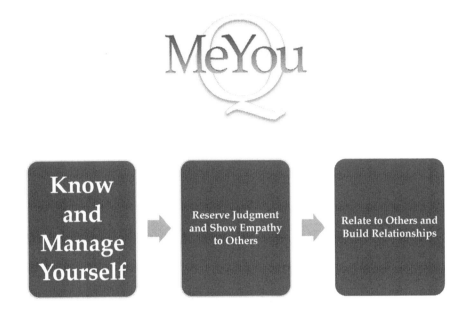

Part 1: Know and Manage Yourself

Why do you do the things you do?

IN THIS PART, YOU WILL DIVE DEEPER into self-awareness, recognizing yourself as a unique individual made up of various traits that you were either born with or developed throughout the years. You will see how behavior tends to be automatic and may not be appropriate for the situation. You will develop a sense of mindfulness about your behaviors, allowing you to decide whether you want to behave a different way in a particular situation. The idea is that many of your traits are fixed, but your behavior is not. You will become comfortable seeing your own patterns and begin to play a more active role in your life.

> **Know and Manage Yourself**
>
> - Recognize yourself as a unique individual with a variety of traits
> - Understand your behavior as a product of your various traits
> - Manage your behavior by consciously choosing your actions

As you prepare to increase self-awareness, consider you have characteristics that describe you when you are by yourself and those that describe you when you are with others. It is important to look objectively at yourself in different situations, so you can see what others see. This part of the book is separated into two sections: You as a SELF and You as an OTHER.

Section 1: You as a SELF

Who do you see when you look in the mirror?

THERE ARE MANY CHARACTERISTICS that make up each of us as individuals, which you see when you are alone and not interacting with anyone. These are your intrapersonal traits. You have personality characteristics (Chapter 1) and experience emotions that may or may not be the same as those experienced by others (Chapter 2). You have a certain level of self-esteem (Chapter 3) and creativity (Chapter 4). You may be prone to anxiety or tranquil and self-assured (Chapter 5). You possess a particular set of values (Chapter 6), have needs and ideas that drive your efforts in certain directions, and personal goals you would like to achieve (Chapter 7). You also have a level of spirituality (Chapter 8) and a feeling of wellness or unwellness (Chapter 9). Through your experiences, you have developed a perspective on life and how things operate in the world (Chapter 10). You have an attitude or outlook that may affect your level of happiness or frustration (Chapter 11). Finally, you have a set of ethics about how people should behave which guides your behavior and influences how you judge others (Chapter 12).

It is important to see all of these aspects of yourself and determine the impact they are having on your behavior. If you can understand yourself better, you will be able to understand others better as well. When you become more mindful about your behavior and what is causing it, you can choose your actions instead of simply reacting. You may also find you operate better in some situations and under certain conditions; by knowing this and choosing your experiences accordingly, you can better set yourself up for positive self-talk, success, and self-confidence.

Continue to read about each of these areas while attempting to understand who you are, how your qualities are affecting your life, and how you can be more mindful about whether you allow these qualities to affect your life. Become aware and remain aware.

Your different traits can be fixed, or change throughout your life, so it's important to re-engage in this process from time to time. The idea is to manage the behavior, not label or judge it. It may be easier to accept a trait than to try to change it; instead of wishing to be different, you can work to embrace the qualities that make you who you are. That is not to say that you shouldn't take a hard look at your traits and try to change the characteristics that aren't serving you where you are able to, but if you are mindful about your reality, you can make a conscious decision on which way to proceed.

Explore each of these areas now and work from recognizing the trait to understanding the influence of the trait on your behavior to management of the behavior.

You as a SELF Takeaways:

↗ *MeYouQ* begins with recognizing the various aspects of your SELF; these are not just your intelligence and your emotions, but so many other things about you

↗ You are a unique individual; embrace that about yourself so you can embrace that about others and build strong, healthy relationships

↗ Be mindful about how your qualities affect your behavior—become aware and remain aware, so you can consciously choose your actions

Chapter 1: Your Personality Type

Did you ever notice that you are more comfortable in certain situations?

YOUR PERSONALITY, WHICH CAN BE measured using tools like the Myers-Briggs Typology Indicator (MBTI), has some characteristics that are relatively unchanging throughout your life. In the MBTI, individuals fall into one of 16 different personality types, which determines how they approach situations in life and what types of situations are favorable to them. While MBTI testing is outside the scope of this book, a short overview of the dimensions of personality on this scale is important because each personality type thrives in certain environments. For example, one personality type is INTJ – Introverted, Intuitive, Thinking, and Judging. Visit www.myersbriggs.org for more information.

- **Introverted-Extroverted:** Introverts can enjoy being around people, but generally re-energize by being alone, while extroverts prefer to spend their time with others, as this is how they recharge. Contrary to old opinion, supervisors don't have to be extroverts to be successful; an introverted supervisor may be especially skilled at quiet reflection and problem solving.

- **Sensing-Intuitive:** Sensors are realists who are practical and want factual information they can gather through their five senses. Sensors think about what is, not what could be. Intuitives are more likely to use their intuition or gut feeling, and think outside the box; they think about strategy and possibilities.

- **Thinking-Feeling:** Thinkers use logic and are impersonal in their reasoning; they focus on rules and may come across to others as cold. Feelers are interested in the opinions and emotions of others, the human side. They are concerned with sensitivity and getting along with others.

- **Judging-Perceiving:** Judgers make a decision and move on; they do not like to be questioned. Judgers are also good at planning and organizing. Perceivers are open to ideas, and may have trouble making decisions due to over-analysis. They are curious and are more accepting of differences.

Recognizing your personality type. If you want to determine your personality type, you can search for a free online test using "16 personalities" or "MBTI free assessment." This book does not go into detail about the 16 different personalities; however, the next part looks at what the different personality dimensions might mean for your behavior. If you find your personality type does not quite describe you, it is likely because you sit more in the middle of the continuum for one or more of the four groupings. The official MBTI would ask more questions and would likely have a more definitive outcome. In any case, you can probably figure out your personality type through reading the descriptions and choosing the one that best describes you.

Go back and read the definitions on pages 16 and 17. Circle the word that <u>best</u> describes you for each pair, recognizing this isn't a scientific method for determining your type:

1. Introvert (I)   Extrovert (E)
2. Sensing (S)   Intuitive (N)
3. Thinking (T)   Feeling (F)
4. Judging(J)   Perceiving (P)

The four letters of your personality are: _____

It is not so much about knowing your exact personality type for *MeYouQ*, it is recognizing that people have different personality types, and these can have a significant impact on behavior. If you know your type, it may be easier to understand your behavior.

Understanding your personality type. Look at the characteristics that describe your personality type, as well as other personality types. At this point some people feel validated and think, "That's why I act that way." As you begin to understand the different dimensions of personality better, you will begin to see that certain situations are more favorable to certain personalities.

Introverts tend to keep to themselves, whereas extroverts are more outgoing. Introverts are more likely to engage in quiet reflection instead of talking a problem out. Extroverts want to jump into a team activity and get busy working on the problem.

People who are sensing are more concerned with what is concrete, real, and practical, while those who are intuitive are more abstract and look for underlying variables in situations. Sensors need to experience a situation, while intuitives can imagine it.

Thinkers do not like to be influenced; they want to analyze the pros and cons of the situation for themselves. Feelers want to know the potential effect of the situation on others, and make the decision based on what is best for the people involved. While a thinker looks for truth, fairness, and logic; a feeler wants harmony, tact, and compassion.

Judgers like it when a decision is made and they feel in control; they make to-do lists and are goal oriented. Perceivers monitor a situation for new information and are open to a change in plans; they may procrastinate until the last minute.

You may go back and change your personality selections now, if this new information caused you to change your mind about your personality type.

Given the above descriptions, you should be able to see the potential for conflict when people with different personalities are working together. Different personality types have very different ways of approaching a situation based on one characteristic, never mind a combination of four. Now let's look at what mindfulness can do to help people in different situations.

Managing your personality type. Because of your personality type, you are going to find some workplace situations more comfortable than others. What is being asked of you at the time might not be the way you naturally tend to or prefer to work. Does that mean you should stay away from those situations, or that you should only work with people who have the same personality as you? No, that would be an unrealistic strategy. It probably means you should consider what the best behavior is for the work required, and determine whether to move away from your natural response. You will not be able to change your personality, but you can change your behavior.

When working as part of a team, you will be able to recognize the different personalities and help determine which team member is best suited to complete each task. Your understanding of personality differences will allow you to accept others and ease tension in the group, helping to ensure members either take on roles suitable to their personality type or adjust their behaviors accordingly.

If you are an *introvert* and you feel uncomfortable in a social situation, you may want to assess your reasons for being there, and, if you choose to stay, how being a little more extroverted could help you to be successful. Try to involve others in your personal reflection; take them through your process. Let them know this is not your preferred situation, but you are working to adapt. If you are an *extrovert* and feel you are getting the wrong vibe from people, you may recognize the situation calls for a little more quiet time and introspection, and less socializing. Give people some time for quiet reflection and be ready to engage with them once they have had their alone time.

If you are a *thinker*, you may feel misunderstood when you are asking the hard questions and people think you are being insensitive. Be careful with how you probe for information as you perform your due diligence. Use tact and sensitivity when you ask questions and respond to input. If you are a *feeler*, do not assume that a group member does not care about people's feelings or harmony in the group; it may be that she is a thinker. Be polite when you point out the people-side of things, and appeal to the thinker's style by offering logical explanations for your points of view.

If you are a *judger*, recognize that your desire to be ahead of things may not be shared by others. Understand that perceivers are more last-minute in their work because they don't want to commit to a course of action too quickly. To work better with perceivers, you may have to be patient and get them to compromise with an earlier deadline for their decision. A perceiver might bring important information to you at the last minute, and you should be prepared to listen. If you are a *perceiver*, you may frustrate others by not completing tasks as quickly as they would like. Be open to committing to a more aggressive timeline than you are comfortable with, and don't get wrapped up in excessive analysis. Communicate with others to ensure that you are all seeing the same information and can agree to the same deadline.

You can work with your personality type to be successful in any situation when you are mindful of how your type may be working against you, and recognize that you are able to choose a suitable action. In Chapter 8, you will delve into the topic of spirituality and mindfulness, but for now, think of mindfulness as being conscious, being aware that there are a variety of influences on your behavior. Personality is just one of them.

(Names of individuals found in this book are taken from the author's friends and family, but are not meant to reflect individual personality

characteristics or the author's opinion of anyone. They are included for fun only.)

> *Deborah makes decisions quickly and doesn't like to sit around in meetings all day. Give her a problem and she will solve it based on how she previously handled a similar situation. She knows the right answer and doesn't need group consultation.*

Deborah's behavior might be frustrating to some people in the organization, and she might have trouble with buy-in from her co-workers. It's likely that she is very knowledgeable and makes good decisions, but it might be necessary to consult others and allow them to participate. If you work to understand Deborah's behavior, you might see it is her personality at play in this situation, not that she thinks she is better than everyone else. She could be *introverted* and do more of her thinking on her own instead of consulting others. She might be a *thinker* and not really stop to consider how others feel. Finally, she might be a *judger* and just want to make a decision and move on.

> *Jim likes to play "what if…?" He is constantly thinking of a way to spin a situation and comes up with crazy scenarios that don't seem possible. "What if this happens? What if that happens?" He loves to brainstorm with others and listen to what they think. Sometimes he comes up with some pretty interesting theories.*

Jim's behavior might annoy some people. His co-workers might be too busy to sit around discussing things that are never likely to happen. What Jim's co-workers may not understand about him is that he has the *intuitive* dimension of personality; he thinks outside the box. He could be *feeling* and really care about what others think in a situation as well. Or perhaps Jim is *extroverted* and gets energized by being around others, regardless of what they are doing.

> *Heather can't commit to a course of action until everyone has been consulted. She wants to make sure she has completely researched a problem and considered all the possible solutions. It seems that she puts off making a decision as long as possible.*

Heather is collaborative, but is all that collaboration really necessary? It could be taking up a lot of time when, in reality, a decision just needs to be made. Maybe Heather is *sensing* and she needs practical information in order to feel comfortable with a decision. Perhaps she is *feeling* and wants to consult others to make them feel like part of the process, or she could be *perceiving* and be prone to over-analysis.

In all of these examples, the individual could come off the wrong way and cause friction with others, or be ineffective in practice. It is important to become aware of how your personality affects your behavior in order to ensure that you are choosing the right behavior for the situation and not letting the behavior choose itself. In each case, the person can work to balance their natural tendency and be more attentive to the people involved. Deborah could develop patience and allot some time to consult with others, realizing the benefits of teamwork and alternate opinions. Jim could tone down his scenarios and keep things realistic. He can be respectful of others' time and space. Heather could scale down the list of people she wants to consult and the amount of information she wants to collect, and give herself a deadline for the decision.

Write an example of a workplace situation that someone with your personality type would be comfortable in. _____

_____

_____

Write an example of a workplace situation that someone with your personality type would be uncomfortable in. _____

_____

_____

For the second example, how could the person adapt to the situation? _____

_____

Build your MeYouQ by knowing your personality type and choosing an appropriate behavior or complementary situation.

Chapter 1 Takeaways:

↗ Your personality type impacts your behavior and certain situations will be more favorable for you

↗ Personality types can be quite different from each other and lead to conflict between individuals because of the way people behave

↗ Staying mindful about the strengths and weaknesses of your personality will help you choose favorable situations, or choose a suitable action, regardless of your natural tendency

Your personality is something built-in and enduring about you, as is the way you handle your emotions. Learning to manage your emotions is another important skill to develop.

Chapter 2: Your Emotions

Do your emotions control you, or do you control your emotions?

RECALL THAT EMOTIONAL INTELLIGENCE is one's ability to recognize when an emotional response may be replacing logical thought in a situation and to choose an action instead of reacting. The original concept of Emotional Intelligence (EQ) was introduced by Daniel Goleman, if you want to do some additional research and self-assessments.

Emotional intelligence is seen as a necessary skill for getting ahead in the workplace. It allows you to be conscious of your emotions and manage them so you can reduce stress, preserve relationships, and recognize when EQ is low in others and might be affecting your interactions.

Emotions occur naturally in people and are difficult, if not impossible, to change, but they can be managed. The emotions you have about a situation can be very different than the emotions someone else has. For example, some people cry when they watch a certain commercial and others don't. Some people get angry in a particular situation and others do not. Even the same event at a different time can elicit a different reaction from you.

If you can't control your emotions, that is, if you have poor emotional intelligence, you might "snap" at people, be upset with them and not know why, or allow your emotions to control your behavior in other ways.

Do you feel that sometimes your emotions take over? Would you like to have more control over them? Would you like to choose your response instead of reacting based on emotion? Explore a few different emotions now, and work from recognizing to understanding to management.

Recognizing your emotions. When someone teases you, can you laugh about it or do you get upset? When a co-worker keeps coming to you for help, do you get annoyed easily? Can any small event send you into a rage? If something bad unexpectedly happens to you, does it send you into despair? Are you easily embarrassed when you do something wrong? Do you feel intense guilt after making a small mistake? In a difficult situation, do you feel defeated and depressed, or do you feel energized and challenged? Regardless of where these feelings originate, the emotion you experience in a situation can cause a productive or non-productive reaction.

If you can learn to recognize the emotions you are having at any given time, you can then work to see how they are affecting, or have the potential to affect, your behavior. You may not be able to stop the emotion, but you can control the response.

Understanding your emotional reaction. Sometimes emotions serve people well, such as when love causes people to do nice things for someone, or fear becomes the motivator for performance. Sometimes emotions take people in the wrong direction. For example, anger about a situation may cause you to dislike someone and to refuse to talk with them again, or

27

frustration may cause you to give up on achieving an important goal. Before you can work to manage your emotions, you need to understand how they might be affecting your behavior. Begin to notice how you behave when you are experiencing different emotions. You may have patterns like telling people to go away or ignoring them when you are under stress, or perhaps you are goofy and do silly things when you are excited about an event. Whatever it looks like, work to understand the connection between your emotions and your behavior.

These behaviors can negatively impact your work relationships if they are not managed. By working to understand how your brain operates, you can be more mindful about the effect your emotions have on you and work to manage your behavior.

Mindful management of your emotions. Once you understand the link between your emotions and actions, you can work to practice effective emotional intelligence. You can choose an appropriate response for the situation, and recognize if the emotion you are experiencing needs attention to resolve.

Sometimes to stop the behavior, you have to block the emotion. This can be difficult if you see the behavior, but you're not immediately sure which emotion is causing it. You may find that journaling will help you to understand why you feel the way you do. For example, you might discover that you are in a bad mood today because of something that happened yesterday. It's only when you can identify the cause of the emotion that you will be able to address the problem. That emotion may continue to affect your behavior until the underlying issue is resolved. You will have to go back to the source and deal with the problem.

In this way you can build resilience and your ability to handle a variety of situations without allowing them to affect your behavior. By not becoming emotional at work, or allowing your emotions to control your behavior, you will be more predictable, more approachable, and more respected.

Danielle is excited about her plans for the weekend. She is quite giddy and is walking around the office visiting everyone and asking what they are doing for the weekend. She's flirting with customers and being a little inappropriate. Her boss has already threatened to send her home without pay.

Natalie's mom and dad recently told her she has to move out on her own in two months. At work, she is being quite short with people when they ask for her help. Her manager asked her what's wrong and she replied that she didn't know.

Katie had a run-in with a customer this morning who yelled at her and then asked to see the manager. Now she is walking around the store gossiping about one of her co-workers. One of her other colleagues mentioned he was surprised she is acting this way, as she is not usually like this.

Eileen might be affected by upcoming layoffs and her finances are not presently in order. She has been busy all day monitoring how much work everyone else is doing and pointing out people who she believes should be let go. She was also bragging to the boss about how well she just handled a difficult customer.

Abby's boyfriend just broke up with her, even though she pleaded for him not to. Today Abby's boss had to correct the way she was folding clothes and Abby burst into tears; then she said she was going to quit because he didn't appreciate her.

In any one of these cases, the person involved likely doesn't realize that her emotions are controlling her behavior. If Danielle could see that she was behaving inappropriately, she might settle herself down and act more professionally. If Natalie could see that her home situation was manifesting as unprofessional behavior, she could be conscious of treating people properly. If Katie did not take things so personally, she would understand that she doesn't have to criticize others in order to feel better about herself. If Eileen realized that she probably can't change the outcome of the pending layoffs by making others look bad, she would stop her self-campaigning at work. If Abby had resilience, she would be able to pick herself up, set her sorrow aside, and continue to function productively. She would think logically about how to deal constructively with her problem. Non-productive behaviors can sure have an emotional component!

Think about a time you reacted in a way you weren't proud of. What was the situation and what was the emotion involved?

_____

_____

In what way was this reaction non-productive for the situation?

_____

If you could have chosen a more appropriate action in this situation, what would it be? _____

_____

Build your MeYouQ by journaling to find emotions that are affecting your behavior and then choosing the appropriate behavior.

Chapter 2 Takeaways:

↗ Emotions have an automatic influence on behavior and you may not notice when your behavior is not in your conscious control

↗ Determining which emotion is affecting your behavior can be difficult, but paying conscious attention to your emotions can help

↗ You might not be able to change the emotion, but with mindfulness you can manage the emotion's effect on your behavior

Many things outside of your immediate awareness can be affecting your emotions and actions, including your self-esteem.

Chapter 3: Your Self-Esteem

Does your internal voice make you doubt yourself?

YOUR SELF-ESTEEM REFLECTS HOW YOU FEEL about your abilities and how much you respect yourself. If you have high self-esteem, you have a feeling of self-worth in that you are accepted by others and are capable of things you consider important. The experiences you have had in life and the stories you tell yourself have formed and continue to form your self-esteem.

People can be successful at work and still have a low self-esteem. It is possible that you are being too critical of yourself, or that you are listening to negative messages from others. If you have low self-esteem you might worry that no one will like you if you do the wrong thing or make a mistake. If people criticize you it might feel like an attack on you as a person. You could be paralyzed against taking action, as you worry about opening yourself up as a target. In this way, your lack of self-esteem can stop you from doing things that will move you ahead in life. Low self-esteem can cause you to think you are wrong about a situation and prevent you from taking action when you need to. Low self-esteem can also mean that you take risks when you shouldn't because you don't care what happens to you.

Overly inflated self-esteem can also be a problem. If you have high self-esteem because you are really good at some things, it would be a mistake to think you are good at everything. If you think you are good at everything, everyone loves you and "it's all about you," people may not like to be around you. In addition, you could be setting yourself up for failure as you take on tasks for which you are ill-suited or unprepared. Keeping your self-esteem in check will help you to be successful in your relationships and in the things you do.

So, how do you know if your self-esteem is getting in the way of your success or your happiness? Explore your self-esteem now, and work from recognizing to understanding to management.

Recognizing your self-esteem. People can have confidence in their ability to handle a situation while still having a low self-esteem. Just because you have confidence in certain situations, it doesn't necessarily mean that you have high self-esteem.

Are you very critical of yourself? Do you find that even after a great success, all you can think about is the tiniest thing you did wrong? When people compliment you on your work, do you allow your self-criticism to overshadow what has been said? Do you have a hard time praising yourself and need others to tell you that you've done a good job? If so, you might have low self-esteem.

Are you the first one to say what a great job you did and how awesome you are? Do you often self-promote to get attention for the things you have done? When working with a team, do you draw attention to the part you played? Do you think you can do no wrong? If so, you might have an over-inflated sense of self-esteem.

Are you able to give yourself a compliment when it's due? Are you ok if you do not get recognition for something you have done? Are you still able to have confidence in your ability after someone has criticized you or you have made a mistake? Are you able to take on new tasks without thinking you are doomed to fail? Are you able to say that you have value as a person regardless of what happens in your life? If so, you likely have a healthy self-esteem.

Understanding your self-esteem. If you can look objectively at your level of self-esteem, you can understand the effect it could be having on your life; how it is currently impacting your behavior.

Someone with low self-esteem can be frustrating to others and to herself. A person with low self-esteem may be unable to take compliments from others and may be continually putting herself down. She might avoid certain situations and be unable to achieve the things in life that she would like to. Her self-doubt or self-criticism can prevent her from taking on a little bit of risk or believing that she deserves things.

Someone with overly high self-esteem is going to alienate others. People will get tired of hearing him brag all the time and of having to give him so much attention. They will also tire of being in his shadow as he takes the credit for a team effort. Someone with overly high self-esteem may think he is doing a great job when he isn't. He might not know what he doesn't know about his job and will think there is nothing he needs to do to improve.

Someone with a healthy self-esteem will respect himself and be confident in his abilities. He will feel like he can take on new challenges and will objectively assess all aspects of his own performance. He will give himself credit for the things he can do, and will work to improve those things that need improvement. He will not need others to make him feel worthy and will accept compliments with a simple "Thank you."

Managing your self-esteem. Self-esteem can change without you even noticing; an event that went really well or really poorly can have an instant impact on your self-esteem. It is important to be mindful about your level of self-esteem, and to notice when it is being affected.

Low self-esteem can cause you to seek attention from others and be unhappy until you get it; you find that positive self-messages are unfulfilling. Alternatively, you may find that even when others compliment you and tell you that you are great, you still have feelings of low self-esteem. Self-esteem is internal in this way, the feedback you get from others may, in fact, do very little to affect this internal state.

Pay attention to what others say about you and what you tell yourself – is the message consistent? Work to develop a realistic picture of yourself, listening to many opinions rather than just a few. Consider the things you have accomplished, and reflect on areas where you have not been as successful; adjust your opinion where necessary. Finally, check in with yourself regularly; the idea is to maintain a realistic sense of self-esteem, rather than one that is inflated or deflated.

Phil feels sorry for himself because he hasn't had a pay raise in three years. He is upset that management hasn't noticed how hard he works. He would ask for a raise, but he's pretty sure the boss would say, "No" because she doesn't like him. Phil would feel stupid if that happened and he doesn't want to set himself up for the disappointment.

Doug plays poker each week and he lets all his friends know how much everyone at work loves him. Apparently, he is the best front-desk employee the hotel has ever had, and his boss adores him. When Doug leaves poker for the night, the guys make fun of him and wonder if he even works at the hotel.

You can see how self-esteem, low or high, can keep people from getting ahead in life and being respected. What's the worst thing that could happen to Phil if he asked for a raise? Is the sky going to come crumbling down? Will suddenly find himself standing naked in the room? He needs to take a more realistic perspective of the situation and make a list of the reasons he deserves a raise. Doug is obviously unaware of how others see him, but how would he ever know? If Doug were to take some time to analyze his personality and how it might be affecting his life, he would have to look at how he represents himself and whether he is embellishing his abilities.

Do you feel you have low, high, or a healthy sense of self-esteem? Do you have the confidence to try new things and feel like you will succeed? _____

_____

_____

Has your level of self-esteem negatively affected your behavior lately? What happened? _____

_____

_____

What could you do to change your level of self-esteem (assuming it's not serving you)? _____

_____

_____

Build your MeYouQ by managing the messages about your abilities and developing a healthy and productive self-esteem.

Chapter 3 Takeaways:

↗ Self-esteem is affected by the stories you tell and hear about yourself; healthy self-esteem is important for success and relationships

↗ When you rely on others to build your self-esteem, you may not have confidence in your own abilities; additionally, compliments from others can get lost as your internal voice drowns them out—balance is required

↗ Having low self-esteem can hold you back, and cause you to miss out on taking opportunities or necessary actions in life

↗ Overly inflated self-esteem can cause others to dislike you, and may mean you end up in situations where you don't have the skills to do the job

↗ To have healthy self-esteem, you should examine your abilities in an objective way, and manage the messages you tell yourself or receive from others

---

While self-esteem can prevent you from taking opportunities, being creative can attract new opportunities.

Chapter 4: Your Level of Creativity

Do you have good ideas, or do you regret them later?

YOUR LEVEL OF CREATIVITY CAN BE an asset, but it can also get you into trouble. Creative people come up with new solutions to problems and ways to innovate new things. These new ideas can be productive or non-productive; for example, innovation can lead some people to pushing the boundaries or breaking the rules.

Your creativity can help you to achieve goals and solve problems. Innovation allows you to produce better tools for your work and improved methods for doing things. Creativity can result in positive changes and bring happiness to you.

However, your level of creativity may cause you to be unhappy with the current state of your workplace because you see the potential to do things differently. You may be pointing out all the things that could be done better and be unable to just accept things the way they are. Your critical approach could prevent you from enjoying your workplace.

Creative people are also more likely to try new things, and sometimes these unproven things fail. The individual may not care about the failure, however, the organization they work for probably does.

A creative person may also have the tendency to change his mind, even after committing to a decision. If this person is a supervisor, employees will become frustrated and uneasy.

Finally, someone can express creativity in the stories she tells. She might embellish the truth in ways that can cause people to mistrust things she says in the future. It would be difficult to see this person as credible.

Explore your own creativity now, and work from recognizing to understanding to management.

Recognizing your creativity. Would you say you are a creative person? Do you find you have many ideas? Have your ideas been successful in the past? Do they cause you to frequently change your mind and jump from one thought or action to the next? What do you get really good ideas about, and which of them have failed?

Are you generally critical of the way things are? Do you spend more time picking apart other people's ideas and systems than following them? Do you spend a lot of time at work criticizing the way things are being done and believe your way would be better?

When you tell a story, does the story change the more times you tell it or depending on who you tell it to? Do people question what you said because they've heard something different from you before? Is your creativity affecting your enjoyment of your work and workplace or the respect you get from others?

Understanding your creativity. Are you able to see the effects of your creativity? Have they been positive, resulting in some really good changes and initiatives? Do you have a reputation for continuous improvement? Do others generally support your ideas?

Has your creativity had a negative effect? Do others get frustrated with you or refuse to go along with your ideas? Are you able to accept other people's ideas, or do you always have to "improve" them? Do you find that others catch you changing your story? Do your ideas cause extra work for those who try to implement them, and result in very little gain? If these statements are true, you are going to have to change the way you are channeling your creativity and manage it in a more positive way.

Managing your creativity. Creativity can be like a running water tap; the ideas just keep flowing out. The creativity tap can be very difficult to turn off, but sometimes it's best to try.

When your creativity is having negative results, you may have to give more consideration to your ideas or decisions before unveiling them to others. Perform your due diligence, so you have thought of as many factors or scenarios as possible, and recognize when an idea just isn't going to bring enough benefit to those involved for the level of change required. You may have to learn to be happy enough with the way things are, and turn off the critical voice in your head. If you find you change your mind too often, train yourself to stick to your decision and only change your mind if there is a compelling reason.

Work to accept the systems that are in place in your organization, for now. Support your organization and work to discuss practices using the appropriate means. Strive to be positive and use positive language, rather than being critical. Recognize that sometimes things are good enough and don't need to be fixed. Just move on to use your creativity elsewhere.

If your creativity is in your stories, pay attention to the stories you tell and whether you are being completely truthful. Do you tend to embellish to create more drama or interest? Be accurate in the words you are using.

Rob has many great ideas and everyone congratulates him for the changes that are implemented at work. Rob becomes resentful that no one else ever has an idea and that he's the one always having to do all the work for these great changes.

Rob's creativity seems like a great thing, but there are some obvious problems. Should Rob just keep his mouth shut and not make suggestions? He is probably starting to feel that way, but that would be a shame. He is going to need to talk to the people in his workplace and see if he can get some help with implementing his ideas. He should expect help if people want these changes, but he should not expect that others have a gift of creativity.

Margaret gets frustrated with her boss's micromanaging. She complains about his many rules and thinks most of them are unnecessary. Last week she got in trouble for leaving work early. She doesn't understand why, as she worked through lunch and all of her work was done. This week, when a customer didn't want to pay full price for a few items, she packaged them together at a special discount rate. She was able to make a sale that she wouldn't have made otherwise, so she can't understand why she is getting a written warning on her file.

It seems that Margaret is working hard and cares about the company. She has good intentions, but she needs to understand that she can't just change things as she sees necessary. If she's disciplined with a warning she might not want to work as hard for the company. To avoid this situation, she could gain pre-approval for her ideas and ensure she is following company policies.

Give an example of the last time you were creative at work and it led to a negative outcome. _____

_____

Describe why you think the creativity was not channeled in the best way. _____

_____

Outline a better way for channeling creativity that would avoid this type of problem. _____

_____

Build your MeYouQ by examining whether your creative thinking is leading to productive outcomes and work to restrain your creativity when it is not.

Chapter 4 Takeaways:
- ↗ Creativity can lead to innovation, improvement, critical thinking, problem solving, and win-win outcomes
- ↗ Creativity can lead to many benefits, but it can also be counterproductive
- ↗ Failure to curb your creativity to an appropriate level can cause you to be unhappy, try too many new things, change your mind, or embellish the truth
- ↗ Sometimes you will have to be ok with the way things are and not try to change them

Your creativity can help you to feel more fulfilled in life, but anxiety will prevent some people from reaching their goals.

Chapter 5: Anxiety Proneness

What can you do to accept and manage your anxiety?

A PERSON WHO IS PRONE TO ANXIETY worries about the unknown. He is unable to take a relaxed approach in a period of change or uncertainty, or when faced with circumstances beyond his control. He tells himself all kinds of stories about what could happen or why the situation is going to be bad.

Too much anxiety in a person's life can manifest as physical symptoms, depression, or other illnesses. It can interfere with your ability to handle things at work, as time is spent worrying about or planning for things that are not likely to happen. Often, the more you think about circumstances that cause you to be anxious, or try to "face your fears" and "just do it," the worse your anxiety becomes. Taking a positive attitude may not be enough to combat the fear, because positivity may not be realistic for the situation. For example, you could convince yourself you are a great public speaker and the audience will love you, when in fact you are an average speaker but can get your point across. Your disappointment in the audience's neutral reaction can result in even more anxiety the next time you speak.

When a person is unable to manage his level of anxiety, he might have inaccurate views of what is going on in the workplace, taking a small issue and turning it into something big.

45

He may worry excessively when there is no reason to. Anxiety doesn't necessarily have to be avoided, but it should be kept at an appropriate level for the situation.

Explore your overall level of anxiety now, and work from recognizing to understanding to management.

Recognizing your level of anxiety. Are you relaxed most time, or do you find yourself becoming anxious in many different situations? Does your inner voice start making excuses for why you can't do something because you want to avoid a seemingly unpleasant situation? Does your mind worry about different outcomes, most of which result in disaster and are unlikely to happen? Alternatively, are you too easy-going and find unpleasant things happen to you because you are unprepared? Do you find others probing you about your plans, when you haven't given much thought to the things they are asking about? Or do you have just enough anxiety to feel in control of a situation; you worry and take precautions, and things usually work out.

Perhaps you are anxious about certain events and calm about others. Maybe you worry more about matters you feel you can control with the right actions, and worry less about those you can't control. Consider all kinds of situations; such as writing tests, thinking about deadlines for projects, wondering how someone feels about you, driving in traffic, and becoming ill. What is your level of anxiety in these situations and how does that affect the actions you take? What are the physical effects the anxiety has on you?

Understanding the impact of your anxiety. Many people are a little apprehensive in a new situation, but does your anxiety paralyze you? Do you find that you cannot let go of your worrying, and it keeps you up at night? Do you feel like you have much stress in your life because of change or unknown outcomes? Alternatively, do you have no anxiety and find yourself ill-prepared for things? Do you just "wing it" and know you could have done a better job? Do people become frustrated with your behavior when you refuse to engage in planning activities with them? Or do you have a healthy method for approaching situations you need to plan for and take part in? Are you able to recognize the things you can change and those you can't? Can you take your fear and channel it into productivity?

Managing your anxiety. Become aware of what your inner voice says to you during a period of change or uncertainty, or when encountering a new situation. Work at challenging the disaster-prediction stories and replacing them with more realistic ones; you don't have to build a positive story, just an accurate one. Gather information about the situation, so you feel empowered instead of victimized. Tell yourself new stories and worry only about the things you can change or impact; if you are anxious about people, work to know them better.

Try to push yourself out of your comfort zone and subject yourself to situations that cause you anxiety—face your fears, even slowly, and just a little bit at a time, so you can maintain an operational level. Try to work through the anxiety by being conscious of how you feel, and build scenarios about what may truly happen. Create new stories about what is going on and your ability to handle the situation.

Carole is a top customer service specialist. The customers love her and rave about her to her boss. She clearly deserves a promotion and has been taking some extra training for the next level in the company which is a position in sales. Carole knows her products inside out and she has studied the role plays over and over again. Her manager has practiced these role plays with her and feels she is ready to work on the sales floor. Carole isn't sure if she's ready; she's never done sales before and knows it isn't easy. On Monday, she was out on the floor talking to a customer, but couldn't recall the sales steps. She ran out crying. She tried again on Tuesday, but froze after the first step. On Wednesday, she couldn't even step out onto the sales floor. She wants to quit and return to her customer service duties where she is confident in her abilities.

It is very sad that Carole's anxiety is holding her back. She knows the sales role and the steps completely. Why is it so hard for her to perform it with a live customer? She is going to have to do something to get over this hump or she will be in customer service forever. Have you ever had anxiety like this? Your brain is telling you, "No" when it is something you thought you were prepared to do. What would you do if you were Carole in this situation? How could you overcome this? Not everyone is able to push past this type of a barrier, and it doesn't even matter how much a person wants to. Perhaps the manager could put Carole in a "safe" sales position, where the customer is not likely to be challenging. She can work up to more complex situations by having small successes. No amount of convincing or encouraging her is working, and a different strategy is needed.

Describe a time you experienced an unrealistic level of anxiety.

_____

_____

What was your inner voice telling you in this instance and how did it affect your behavior? _____

_____

_____

If you could choose a different story to tell yourself in this situation, what would you say? _____

_____

If you could choose a new behavior in this situation, what would you do? _____

_____

Build your MeYouQ by recognizing when your anxiety level is unrealistic and holding you back, while taking small steps to overcome real anxiety so you can be effective in the situation.

Chapter 5 Takeaways:

↗ There is no point worrying about things you can't control

↗ The right amount of anxiety can motivate you to take action when necessary

↗ Too much anxiety may prevent you from seeing the real situation; you might spend time worrying instead of taking productive action

↗ A positive approach that tells you to ignore the anxiety may not work; a realistic approach may be better for you

↗ Anxiety can lead you to have an unrealistic view of what is going to happen; too much of this type of anxiety can cause health problems

↗ Stop and think about the small steps you can take to overcome your anxiety; ignoring it might not be prudent

Hopefully, you are able to develop a method for overcoming any anxiety you experience. Maybe this will be easier when the work you are doing is in line with your values.

Chapter 6: Your Lifelong Values

Do you consciously choose activities that match your values?

YOUR VALUES TELL YOU what is important in life and impact what you work toward, the direction of your efforts. Values are ingrained in people and are generally fairly stable. It would take a major life event to change your values.

When people choose work and activities congruent with their personal values, they have more peace and passion than when they are engaging in work that conflicts with their values. If you had to go to work every day to do something you didn't believe in, it would have a negative impact on you. Someone valuing honesty would have a hard time using questionable sales tactics, for example.

People seek work arrangements that help them achieve what is important to them. Someone who values family will find it difficult to be away from home, but will work hard to provide a steady income. Someone valuing money will work hard for the monetary reward. Someone valuing leisure will make sure to use their vacation days.

If you can find an organization and work environment with values that complement your own, you will be more engaged at work and realize more peace and completeness in your life. If your work environment is not a good fit, you will experience stress and won't be engaged.

Have you considered your values and the impact they have on the choices you make? Do you consciously seek out experiences that are in line with your values? Explore your values now, and move from recognizing to understanding to management.

Recognizing your values. Common values include: autonomy, balance, compassion, challenge, citizenship, community, fairness, faith, fame, fun, growth, honesty, justice, ethics, learning, peace, respect, security, spirituality, success, and wealth. Values guide behavior, while they also describe the end state a person would like to achieve.

Many websites have lists of values to aid you in identifying those that apply to you. Select five or six principles that resonate with you; the ones you feel are the most important goals for your life. What are you the happiest doing? Can you connect those things to the values on your list?

Understanding your values. Articulating your values will help you to see what drives you and why you are drawn to some situations while avoiding others. If you are conflicted or stressed at work, you may notice that what you are being tasked with is not in line with your values. For example, if you value hard work and continuous improvement, but most people at your workplace are lazy and unwilling to improve, this is not going to be a healthy work environment for you. You will struggle with being there each day and will probably feel like you should be lazy too, but you won't compromise your values.

If you value helping others, a favorable work arrangement for you would be one where you assist people in need, such as nursing, teaching, or social work. To be really passionate and engaged at work, it's important to see the connection between your values and your work situation. Where possible, put yourself in environments that are compatible with your values.

Managing your values. Organizations have values as well. If your personal values collide with those of the company, you are going to experience stress and disengagement. Careful consideration of who you are going to work for can go a long way in determining your future happiness and success.

You may love your organization and what it stands for, but the role you play there conflicts with your values. Your co-workers may also do things that clash with your values. Work to recognize that the stress you have at work could be caused by a values conflict. You can recognize it as that and deal with the stress or, where possible, you can change your situation. Try not to let the circumstance affect your mood or attitude as you work to solve your problem. Recognize that while it is difficult for you to change your values, it is also difficult for others to change theirs.

Paul values his leisure time. There isn't a weekend where you won't find him out fishing on the lake or puttering in his garage. His boss would like to give him a special project that will develop some skills needed for a promotion, but Paul just isn't interested. This frustrates his boss because he sees so much potential in Paul. He becomes upset with Paul and starts giving him the less desirable jobs around the shop.

Dan values knowledge. He is on several committees, and people always come to him for information. Some would say he has power because he knows many things that others don't. Dan's boss would like to send him out on the road as a salesman, which would mean that he wouldn't be able to sit on these committees anymore. He doesn't care about the extra money he would earn, and is thinking of quitting his job if his boss takes him out of the office.

Susy values family and asked, a week in advance, for a day off to go on a field trip with her son and his class. Her boss denied her request because it's too busy a time of the year. Susy called in sick that day so she could go on the trip.

Owen values money. He will take any extra shift to earn the tips and additional pay. His boss asked him if he would be on the social committee for the next year, as everyone needs to take a turn. Owen is not at all interested in this, and doesn't even participate in these social events. He and his boss are in a big argument about it, and she is threatening to take away his extra shifts if he doesn't cooperate.

We all have values that others may not recognize or understand. Values are important drivers in a person's life. However, while it would be nice to only do the things that appeal to your system of values, life doesn't always work like that; some compromise is usually required. How can Paul's boss entice him into the extra learning while still ensuring he gets his leisure time? How can Dan arrange his work so that he can still be part of the committees he enjoys and have access to information like he is used to? How can Susy get family accommodation and still do her work? Should Owen be forced to be on the social committee, or can he be on another committee that is more in line with the things he likes to do?

If you can arrange to be in situations that appeal to your values most of the time, consider yourself pretty lucky. If you are placing people into positions in your organization, it is important to know what their values are, so they can be allocated accordingly.

Write down one of your values. _____

Give two examples of how this value has led you to take on a certain role or set a goal in your life. _____

_____

_____

Give two examples of situations where this value clashed with a role you were asked to play. _____

_____

_____

Give two examples of situations (in any workplace, not just the one you are currently in) that would be ideal for you based on this value. _____

_____

_____

Build your MeYouQ by recognizing that your comfort level and sense of purpose will be enhanced when you are in an organization or position compatible with your values.

Chapter 6 Takeaways:

↗ Knowing your values will allow you to choose compatible situations and enhance your comfort, peacefulness, and passion

↗ Different people can have different values; it doesn't mean they are wrong, it means different things are important to them

↗ Stress and conflict at work could be due to people having different views of what's important in life; be able to see this and work to move past these differences

↗ Values are enduring; you don't need to change your values and you shouldn't expect others to change theirs

Some people get values confused with needs. Your values are inherent principles that govern how you live, while your needs will change more frequently based on where you are at in life.

Chapter 7: Your Underlying Needs

How do your needs drive your behavior?

PEOPLE NEED CERTAIN THINGS TO SURVIVE and grow in life, including a place to live, nourishment, and physical contact. They also have needs that are more personal, for example, to feel valued and accepted by others, or to feel a sense of challenge and growth. Throughout their lives, people strive to fill the void created by some need. They do this by defining what they want in life, such as a fancy vehicle, a certain career, a specific level of income, or a family; wants are how individuals attempt to fill their needs.

Needs are your drivers in life, and they are changing all the time. If you didn't have these drivers, you wouldn't seek to do anything at all. They can move you in a healthy direction or an unhealthy one. For example, a person's brain may tell her that she needs to get high, so she decides she wants to buy drugs instead of wanting the natural high achieved through a positive or fun experience. A person's brain may tell him he needs power, so he decides he wants to be a thief, but there are legitimate ways to gain power without harming others. If you let your needs drive your wants without consciously thinking about them, you could get yourself into real trouble!

Needs will drive your behavior until they are fulfilled, then other needs will appear. You may be trying to fulfill several needs at once, and those needs could be conflicting with each other. Pay attention to your needs and how they are affecting your behavior. Look at examples of your behavior and understand the specific needs that could be driving it; decide if there is a better way to fulfill the need. Often there are different, healthier, or more productive options available.

People often have a difficult time defining their needs. They feel a discomfort and know they're not happy, but they don't know why; they are yearning for something in their life, but they don't know what. This may cause people to take on different tasks or roles that they think will satisfy them, only to find they are still dissatisfied because the need has not been met. For example, a person signs up to be on a committee and then resents having to go to meetings. What need were they trying to meet by joining that committee in the first place? It is important to take the time to first identify your needs and then decide how best to fulfill them.

Explore your needs now, and work from recognizing to understanding to management.

Recognizing your needs. What discomforts are you feeling right now? Are you unhappy with the work you are doing? Are you bored with your social group? Do you want to go shopping all the time? These feelings and desires are an indication of your needs.

Have you consciously thought of what your needs are and how to best fulfill them? Are you concerned with earning more money? What are you hoping the money does for you? Are you trying to get attention or appreciation from others? This might be a social need that isn't fulfilled for you. Are you unhappy in your job? Explore what it is specifically that you are not happy about, is it really your job, or is there an underlying need that ultimately has nothing to do with work. You might find there is a way to satisfy the need without having to quit your job.

Have you ever been in a situation where you thought you wanted to do or to have something, but once you achieved or attained it, it didn't end up satisfying you? Many people don't know why they do what they do. It's as if they are blindly grabbing anything that seems interesting, but they are not paying attention to the needs they have, so the activity doesn't end up being gratifying. When people regularly identify their needs, they can choose the actions that will be the most rewarding.

Understanding your needs. Some of your needs may have been with you your whole life. You may have a need to help others, to work autonomously, to be in charge, to help the environment, to have stability, to be entrepreneurial, to have balance in your life, or to be challenged in your work. These enduring needs have pushed you in the direction of where you are today and are linked to your values.

At any given time, you can also have the need to be accepted by a group, to grow in your ability, to be appreciated, to make more money, to have a new place to live, to appear more attractive, or one of countless other needs. In each of these cases, there are multiple ways of fulfilling the need. Consider the decisions you have made and the directions you have gone in your life, and identify the need or needs you have been trying to fulfill. Once you uncover your needs, you can assess whether you have been doing the right things to meet them.

Managing your needs. It's not so much that you can manage your needs, but you can manage how you try to satisfy them. Try to put more thought into the actions you take to understand why you are moving in a particular direction and identify the need you are attempting to satisfy. If you analyze the situation and what it is going to do for you, and only say, "Yes" to things that will satisfy you, you will be better able to meet your needs and you will feel less discomfort in your life. Is this starting to sound like WIIFM?

Realize, however, that you should help others to fulfill their needs as well, so you cannot always choose actions based only on whether it is the best way to fulfill your own need. Managing your needs means you are making deliberate choices by recognizing the need being presented and assessing situations carefully to see if they are going to fulfill the pressing need, yours or someone else's.

> *Elaine is a leader. People are always asking for her help, inviting her to chair different committees and take on extra responsibilities. Elaine loves making people happy, so she doesn't say, "No," when asked. Lately, however, she is becoming resentful that no one else is doing as much as she is. She is considering quitting her job because she is overworked and being taken advantage of.*

If Elaine were to take a look at her needs, she might see that her prominent need at this time is not a social one. She is saying, "Yes" to these extra things because she does not want to upset people and because she likes making them happy, but this people-pleasing is really doing nothing for her. She may actually want to learn something new, or start her own business, but she is allowing other people to dictate her actions. She should manage her behavior in order to best fulfill her own needs, rather than those of others.

What was the last extra activity you signed up to do? _____

_____

What need are you expecting to fill with this activity? _____

_____

_____

If you could go back and re-decide whether to participate in this activity, in light of being more aware of your needs, would you make a different choice? _____

What would be a better activity to fulfill this particular need? (Assuming the first was not a good choice.) _____

_____

Build your MeYouQ by discovering the relationship between your actions/activities and your inherent drive to fulfill certain needs.

> **Chapter 7 Takeaways:**
> ↗ You have needs that drive and motivate your actions in life; these change frequently, so work on becoming aware and remaining aware of your needs
> ↗ Needs can be satisfied in different ways; it's important to be conscious and make good decisions about the actions and activities you are choosing
> ↗ It may be difficult to identify your most pressing needs; you may have to look at the activities you are excited about and those you aren't, and work backwards to figure it out
> ↗ Learn from the bad experiences you've had by recognizing how they didn't work to fulfill your needs

Some people have a need for spirituality in their lives and they don't realize it. If you feel something is missing in your life, it could be that you have a disconnect in this area.

Chapter 8: Your Feelings of Spirituality

Do you consider yourself spiritual? Is it even on your radar?

YOUR SPIRIT MAY NOT BE SOMETHING to which you have given much attention. Most workplaces have not been very good at having a holistic approach, that is, caring for mind, body, and soul. Your mind can be cared for by meeting your needs and reducing your stress; your body is cared for by keeping you safe on the job; your soul, however, seems to be left for you to care for on your own.

Spirituality is a way to get in touch with your soul-side. It can help you connect with the innermost part of you, who you were before you developed the thoughts and feelings influenced by your environment and experiences. Some people associate spirituality with religion, but others see it as something deeper than this, a connection to universal energy. Different people use different tools, or approaches, for connecting to their soul, or spirit, or essence.

A great tool for approaching spirituality is mindfulness—the skill you have been practicing with the recognition, understanding, and management of your traits. Mindfulness is being *present* in your thoughts and experiences, living in the moment, and not dwelling on regret about the past or anxiety about the future. Being mindful allows you to recognize that you

63

can only control your current situation; that is, what is happening now. The ego is the voice of regret and worry, and it does not always give an accurate message. Mindfulness helps you to ignore the chatter of the ego and prevent those negative messages from affecting your reality.

You may not be interested in studying or learning about spirituality, but try to keep an open mind about what it might be able to offer you. Explore your spirituality now, and work from recognizing to understanding to management.

Recognizing your spirituality. If you have never thought about your spirituality you might think you lack it altogether; you feel no connection to something larger than yourself. It can be difficult for some people to imagine that they are part of something greater, some larger energy source or being. If you grew up influenced by religion, you may already feel your connection to a higher power, to your God. If not, you may have to do some work in order to accept the possibility.

There are some great books out there that talk about archetypes or being powerful in the now. Whether you agree with the concepts or not, these types of books can be useful for you to see that developing a spiritual mindset can be a very healthy way for people to deal with life's hardships.

When you become more spiritual, you will feel a stronger connection to your essence, passion, and heart. It will feel like a weight has been lifted off your shoulders. Spirituality gives you permission to be yourself and live your life's purpose. You will have more peace and love as you move away from the negative voice in your mind, and see yourself as full of potential and positivity.

Understanding your spirituality. It may be frustrating you that some people have a strong connection to their spirit and you feel you have none. The human brain, or ego, and having grown up in an age of science, can cause people to demand proof for everything; if they can't see or touch something, it doesn't exist. With spirituality, you won't have the proof until you become more spiritual.

If you can challenge yourself to see all sides of things and open your mind to new possibilities, it is going to help you in life. If you are not at all spiritual, that is ok; it is something you can work to understand the benefits of, even if you cannot embrace it completely. Given that so many people believe in a larger purpose or something bigger than themselves, maybe there's something to it. Talk to people about their beliefs and you will find there are many different thoughts and theories, some you will agree with and some you won't. If you find something that works for you, that's great. If you don't, keep trying.

Managing your spirituality. If you feel as though you don't have a spirit and can't believe you are connected to everything else and are here on earth for a reason, that's ok. Many people feel that way. You can still use the principles of spirituality to help you manage stress in a healthy way. Practice meditation to slow yourself down, focus on your breathing and push the worry out of your mind. Say the mantra "calm" as you breathe in and again as you breathe out. Calming your mind this way allows you to take time to appreciate what is happening in the moment, so you can devote your full attention to a person or a problem. You will also be better able to remove negative thoughts of regret over past mistakes and instead recognize what you can learn from those experiences, and how you could handle them differently next time.

Take the attitude that everything you have been through in your life was for a purpose. You were exactly where you were supposed to be to learn the lesson you needed to learn. You had that particular upbringing to make you the person you are today; it had to be that way—you had to go through those things. You are with the people you are with today because they have something to teach you. It can be difficult to see this at the time, but trust it is true. Forgive yourself for the mistakes you have made; you are human. Don't worry about the future; worry is a waste of energy and what you fear may not even happen. Be present in the moment.

Shauna is out at a networking lunch with her mentor. They are talking about how things have been going and her mentor is telling stories about "back in the day." Shauna can't stop her mind from wandering. She is the same age as her mentor; she should be in his position by now. Why did she wait so long to go back to school and start her career? She begins to resent her husband for putting his career ahead of hers. She wonders if she should have ever had children. She worries that there is no possible way she will ever be able to reach the goals for her career that she has in mind; she just doesn't have enough time left to work and she has to still look after the kids and make dinner at night and clean the house and do laundry and... and... and...

Wow, Shauna has some issues going on! There are many Shaunas out there. People who can't get centered, people who are hung up on regret from the past and who worry incessantly about the future. Shauna needs to slow things down and reflect on what is happening in the present, while managing anxiety about her future, as was discussed in Chapter 5.

One view of spirituality would tell Shauna that everyone is here for a reason and she is exactly where she is supposed to be in her career. The lessons that she has learned in life and the experiences she has had have all brought her to where she is today; she had to go through all of those things to do what she needs to do next. The future will also unfold the way it is supposed to.

Another view of spirituality would tell Shauna she can only control what is happening right now. She can't worry about the past because there is nothing she can do to change it. She can plan for the future, but it may or may not come to fruition. All Shauna can really do is live in the moment, and if she does that, she will notice all the wonderful things that are going on around her.

There are many other views of spirituality, but hopefully you can see how these types of beliefs or philosophies can influence how people manage their thoughts in a positive way. People without a spiritual perspective might be more like Shauna in her lunch date scenario.

Examine your spirituality. Are you a Shauna? Write down your beliefs about your spirit. _____

_____

_____

Give an example of how your lack of spirituality has failed to serve you in the past. _____

_____

_____

Given this situation, what could you do differently next time if you take a more spiritual approach? _____

_____

_____

_____

Build your MeYouQ by caring for your spirit
and reducing your feelings of
regret and worry by managing the
thoughts you give your attention to.

> **Chapter 8 Takeaways:**
> ↗ Remember to take a holistic approach to managing your life by caring for your mind, body, and soul
> ↗ Connecting to something larger than yourself may not seem natural, but it will give you a different, and healthy, perspective about the world
> ↗ Recognize your mind (ego) working against you; push the messages of regret and worry away, as you concentrate on what is happening in the present moment
> ↗ Seek further knowledge about spirituality, and try using some form of meditation for its great benefits in slowing down your thinking

If spirituality is not a void for you, perhaps you have a feeling of unwellness in another area of your life.

Chapter 9: Your Feeling of Wellness

When was the last time you felt really great?

HUMAN WELLNESS COMES IN SEVERAL categories: health, financial, spiritual, and social, just to name a few. Each of these requires us to take care of ourselves in different ways. In some cases you may not have control over all of these areas, and you may have to cope with your reality. Attempting to change or cope with your situation may require you to engage in a balancing act to ensure you can meet all the demands you face. This isn't always easy. Pressure in one area may mean other areas suffer.

You may be suffering from an illness or disability which can affect your overall outlook on life, perhaps making it difficult to be positive and cheery. You may have financial or family issues that affect you on a daily basis, causing you to be easily distracted at work and unable to apply yourself completely to your job. You may be subject to a home or work environment that impacts you negatively and has an overarching impact on your ability to live a *normal* life.

There are all kinds of ways people feel well or unwell. It is good to have a look at the factors that are affecting your life and determine how they are impacting you. Explore the effects of different circumstances in your life on your feelings of wellness now, and work from recognizing to understanding to management.

Recognizing your feeling of wellness. What is bothering you in your life right now? Sometimes people feel like something is weighing on them and they don't know what the exact cause is. It could be something more than the unfulfilled needs discussed in Chapter 7. Look at all of the aspects of your life – finances, physical health, mental health, relationships, social circle and community, occupational, intellectual – and see what resonates with you. Have you been arguing with your significant other, bothered by something going on? Is it your job, the organization, or the atmosphere in the workplace? Do you have demands on your life such as kids or pets that are just becoming too much? Have your friends or family been a source of conflict? Have you not been feeling physically well? Do you feel depressed without knowing why? Do you feel unmotivated and lost in your life, wondering if there is something you are missing in the big picture? Are you having financial troubles?

See if you can determine the source of your discomfort. You may have to write in a journal to uncover what is really bothering you. Keep at it until you come up with very specific causes.

Understanding your feeling of wellness. Once you narrow down one or more possible causes of the feeling of unwellness in your life, you can work to see the effect it's having on you. While you might feel your job is too stressful or people around you are too demanding, when you really think about it and discover the source of your discomfort, it could be something else causing you to feel unwell. Similarly, as you work to understand your emotions and their effect on your behavior (as discussed in

71

Chapter 2), you can also look at specific areas that affect your general well-being. What is causing the feelings you are experiencing?

Women have a somewhat predictable feeling of unwellness around a certain time of the month. A surge of emotions sneaks up on most women a day or a few days before their period begins. These hormone-induced emotions can cause women to be moody and they may weep or lash out. Most women do not have an immediate awareness of what is going on, but then their period starts and it becomes obvious in retrospect. If you have this surge of emotion, work to understand your feeling of unwellness as being related to hormones (if you do not have this surge of emotions, work to understand that this could be affecting those that do).

For any feeling of unwellness, once you know what the source is, look at the risk of ignoring it and just hoping it goes away. Also think about whether you are willing to allow this feeling to continue. Is it worth it to you to pursue change? What are the consequences if you don't? Many people think they are trapped in a situation, but they can empower themselves to take control and seek a solution. The source of the discomfort, however, must first be determined.

Managing your feeling of wellness. If you decide to seek a solution, be prepared to work with others in your journey. Be able to tell people what you need, and ask for their help. Be prepared to get out of your comfort zone and stretch yourself in some way. The way you have been handling things is not working, so you have to change what you do. Most problems do not go away on their own, it takes diagnosis and implementation of a solution. If you are physically or mentally unwell, go see a doctor. If you are having financial troubles, talk to a money coach or financial planner. If you are having conflict with someone, you may need to resolve it or have some time apart.

Try not to take your feelings of unwellness out on others. People don't know what is going on with you and they won't understand your behavior. Even if they did, it does not mean you can treat people poorly. Let them know that you are working on a personal issue and that you should be ok soon. You don't have to offer an explanation if you do not want to, but consider that people may be able to better support you if you do. Don't be afraid to ask for help.

Once you have things in order, continue to be aware of your feelings of wellness so you will recognize it should the symptoms return. Understand the potential consequences of ignoring the feeling and continue to deal with the issues you are facing.

Terri has felt a little off lately, but thinks it's probably just her hormones. She comes into the office, but is just not providing the level of attention and care to her work that she usually does. Customers begin to notice and they ask if something is wrong. She hadn't really noticed that her work was being affected. When she thinks about it, she has never had hormones do this to her before. She isn't aware that anything is bothering her; she just doesn't feel like herself.

If Terri allows herself some time for introspection, she should be able to work backwards to identify what is bothering her. She realizes that she hasn't been sleeping well for the last month and has canceled out on a couple of social events. She wonders if something is wrong with her physically and decides to deal with the situation now. She makes an appointment to talk to her doctor about her issue.

Deanna and Raymond argue about money a lot. They are both working, but they can't seem to get ahead financially. Deanna worries about the credit card debt that Raymond is not paying off. Even though they have separate accounts, it bothers her that Raymond is so irresponsible with money. At work, she teases people for going out for lunch all the time and wasting their money. It's really starting to annoy her that people can't handle their finances.

Deanna's views on money are causing some stress for her. Do other people's spending habits really affect her own financial wellness? At work probably not, but at home it might. Deanna is probably allowing things to bother her that shouldn't because she has this problem looming at home. Raymond's credit card debt might affect her if Raymond can't afford to go on a vacation with her, or pay his share of the bills, and if this is a realistic worry, then she should talk to Raymond about it. If it really has nothing to do with her, she needs to understand that she has no control over the situation. Either way, she can work towards feeling better.

Do you have a feeling of unwellness? List some things that may be causing it. _____

_____

_____

How is this affecting you? _____

_____

_____

Is this something you should attend to? What can you do, if anything? _____

_____

_____

Build your MeYouQ by searching for the cause of any feeling of unwellness and asking for assistance while you work through it to get better.

> **Chapter 9 Takeaways:**
> ↗ Your overall feeling of wellness depends on a variety of factors, including health, financial, spiritual, and social
> ↗ You might have feelings of unwellness because you are ill, you live or work in an unfavorable environment, or for another reason related to money, friends, family, or job; something is causing you to feel "off"
> ↗ People aren't always aware of why they feel unwell; look at all of these aspects of your life to identify what's wrong
> ↗ Seek help for your problems as they may not get better on their own; ask others to understand and be patient with you

The issues causing your unwellness may be rectified if you look at where your habits and expectations in those areas come from. These can be found in your previous experiences.

Chapter 10: Your Previous Experiences

How much are you allowing your past to affect your future?

YOU WERE RAISED IN A CERTAIN family, went to certain schools, did different activities in your spare time, worked at different jobs, had different friends, and participated in many events in your life. Each of these unique experiences has impacted you one way or another, a little bit or profoundly. No one else has the exact same history as you.

Each person's life experience will shape their values, beliefs, views, intelligence, preferences, and ways of doing things. You cannot change your history, but you can work to recognize how it is impacting what you do now, and make conscious choices about how you allow it to affect you.

Explore the effects of your previous experiences now, and work from recognizing to understanding to management.

Recognizing the effect of your previous experiences. What were your parents like? Were they permissive or disciplinarian? Did they spoil you or make things tough? Did you have siblings, and how were you treated compared to them? Did you grow up in a happy household with many fun experiences, or was the experience miserable? Did your family have money for you to do things, or were you poor?

What were the kids like in school? Did they accept you, or were you teased? Were you part of the popular group? How did your teacher treat you? Were you smart in class, or did you struggle? Did people gravitate toward you, or ignore you? Were you into sports, cars, video games, or books?

Did you work early in life? Did you babysit, or have a paper route? When you worked for someone else did they like you, or were you fired? What were their expectations compared to yours? Were they patient with you on the job, or did they get upset easily?

Did you push boundaries, or did you obey authority? Did you get into trouble? Did you learn any hard lessons that you had to pay for in some manner? Did people respect you, or were you considered a trouble-maker? Did you grow up participating in decision making, or were you never permitted to make decisions for yourself?

Were people nice to you throughout your life, or have you been mistreated? Do you relate well to others or do you have issues communicating? Are you used to having things provided for you, or have you had to fight for everything you've received?

All of these experiences, and many others, affect your thoughts, choices, and behaviors. The treatment you received may have affected who you grew up to be or what you grew up to do. You internalized all of these messages and they impacted how your sense of self was formed.

Understanding the effect of your previous experiences. People who were treated well and had everything they needed are going to see things differently than people who had an unfortunate upbringing. People who were overindulged are going to see things differently as well.

If you were spoiled growing up, you might expect that things be given to you without you really having to work for them. When things don't work out now, you might blame others instead of looking at your role in the situation. The consequences of or what you were told about your behavior, might have given you the perspective of an external locus of control, where you blame others for what happens to you and take no ownership. Someone with an internal locus of control ("I determine my own fate") would feel accountability and look at what she could do better next time. It is important to see whether you had a role in a situation and take responsibility when appropriate and necessary.

Maybe you grew up having a lot of control over what you were able to do, and now you tend to challenge authority in the organization you work for. This view of entitlement is generally not realistic for life as an adult, where you will have to work hard for everything you get and play fair with others.

If you were treated poorly, or if you were not the popular kid growing up, you may have developed a "chip on your shoulder," which causes you to do whatever you want to do, even if it hurts others. Other people are always hurting you, so who cares, right? You might fight to get your way, because you've had to fight for everything you ever got. Maybe no one ever gave you attention, so you create drama to get some now.

If you were treated well, you probably treat others well too. You are probably generous and supportive because that's what you were taught. Even if you were financially poor, you may have had a wonderful experience with the people around you. You might, however, have trouble relating to those who didn't have a good upbringing. You might not be empathetic to their experiences and the effect of those on them.

In all of these situations, it is important to take ownership, to see that something in your past may be affecting your behavior in a negative way, but to also gain consciousness. Awareness of how your experiences are affecting your life can help you to manage your actions and also aid you in understanding the experiences of others.

Managing the effect of your previous experiences. If life is going along just swimmingly for you, that's great! Count your blessings and continue to have wonderful relationships. The term "pay it forward" means you don't have to repay everyone who does something nice for you, but you can do something nice for someone else. Be a contributor to someone else's positive experience. Treat everyone well, and work to understand others and how their experiences could be affecting their behavior and impacting your relationship with them. Help them to recognize, understand, and manage their personal experiences.

If you engage in disagreements that get out of control, step back and examine your behavior. Are you imitating what happened to you in the past? Is there a better way to operate in the situation? Do you need to get some help with your communication skills? Do you have realistic views about the situation? Maybe the other person is the one at fault, but is there something you can do to help them be a better communicator, or have a more realistic view of the circumstances? This is looking at the situation in the present and not under the undue influence of the past.

Whatever the situation, if it doesn't seem to be going the way you would like, take an objective look at how your past experiences could be affecting your ability to cope now. You can't manage your actions if you aren't aware of their origin.

Joe was brought up in a large family. If they didn't rush to the dinner table and get their food quickly, they might not get any at all. Dinner was fun and energetic, with everyone talking at the same time, interrupting each other to share their stories. Joe's mother was very busy and his older siblings often had to look after him. He learned to play baseball and climb trees out in the backyard.

Joe recently had his performance review at work, and he is being put on notice for his rudeness. He often interrupts people in meetings and is always first in line when the food arrives. After meetings and at the end of the day he is the first one out the door to go home. He never helps with anything extra.

It looks like neither Joe nor his boss has any idea about the impact Joe's childhood has had on him. No one taught Joe to wait his turn and not interrupt others. It was *every man for himself* at Joe's house, and he's carried that into his work life. Joe will need to develop his work manners quickly if he is going to keep his job, and his boss should recognize that he might need a little help in adapting. Joe's behavior is not excusable, but it is understandable.

List one thing about the experiences you have had in your life that might be impacting you now in some way, and describe the impact. _____

_____

What do you need to do to lessen the impact of this previous experience on your current life? _____

_____

How will this help you improve your life? _____

_____

List another thing about the experiences you have had in your life that might be affecting you now, and describe how it's impacting you. _____

_____

What do you need to do to lessen the impact of this previous experience on your current life? _____

_____

How will this help you improve your life? _____

_____

Build your MeYouQ by becoming aware of the impact your history is having on your current behavior, and work to break any behaviors that aren't serving you.

Chapter 10 Takeaways:

↗ Your own unique personal history and past experiences help to form your outlook on life and affect your thoughts, choices, and behaviors

↗ If you developed an external locus of control, you may have difficulty accepting blame or credit; if you have an internal locus of control, you can more easily take credit and accept responsibility for your actions

↗ Your past can impact your expectations of others and what you feel you are entitled to

↗ You may not realize your behavior is an imitation of the way someone treated you in the past

↗ Being conscious about how your past experiences might be affecting you now will help guide you more appropriately

It is possible your attitude also comes from a previous experience, perhaps from a parent or other influence in your life.

Chapter 11: Your Attitude

Do you regularly choose your attitude for the day?

YOUR ATTITUDE DETERMINES HOW you will respond to events in your life. Do you typically see things in a positive light or a negative one? Do you believe the glass is half full (optimism) or the glass is half empty (pessimism), or do you not care either way (ambivalence)? These attitudes can come from many different aspects of your personality that have already been discussed, including your experiences, your ability to handle your emotions, and the level of spiritual awareness you have.

Your attitude is important in determining your happiness and whether you will be able to work well with others. If you focus on negative things and have a pessimistic or ambivalent attitude, you may become depressed or have difficulty seeing the potential for joy in things. Others might not like being around you either.

According to the law of attraction, like attracts like, therefore people will attract what they present, or pay attention to. If they focus on the negative, they will notice negative details, give off negative energy, and as a result more negative things will happen. If they can focus on the positive, they will recognize and appreciate positive things, exude positive energy, and consequently more positive things will happen. That is not to say that you should not be realistic about a situation if it is a negative one, but for the most part if you look for the bright side of things you will be happier, get along better with others, and attract more positive things into your life.

Explore your attitude now, and work from recognizing to understanding to management.

Recognizing your attitude. How do you usually look at a situation? Positively or negatively? With optimism, pessimism or ambivalence? Are you a complainer or gossiper, or do you look at the bright side and give people the benefit of the doubt? Do people usually smile and want to engage with you, or do they avoid you and return to work? These reactions might be a clue as to the type of attitude you have, but you should be able to take an objective look at yourself and recognize it as well.

When you woke up this morning, were you grouchy, did you find it difficult to get out of bed? Did the other drivers or transit passengers annoy you? How did you relate to the people you came into contact with today? Were you friendly and helpful, or did negativity spew out of your mouth? Did you use manners, or were you rude? Were you patient, or were you annoyed with others? Is this normal behavior for you?

Can you catch yourself with a negative attitude? Can you work to see how your mood, happy, grumpy, or sad, affects others around you? Can you see that it can affect your mental health as well? Work to be aware all the time.

Note that chronic unhappiness and pessimism can be a sign of mental illness. Please seek medical advice if this describes you, and know that it is not a sign of weakness.

Perhaps you woke up on the "right side of the bed" with a positive attitude. You enjoyed your morning routine as you got yourself ready for the day. On the way to work, you engaged in light conversation with others or let someone cut into the lane in front of you. When you arrived, you said, "Good morning" to your co-workers and approached your workday with energy and interest.

If you adopted an attitude of ambivalence for the day, you probably didn't put much thought into what you put on for clothes or ate for breakfast. You traveled to work without noticing much around you. When you arrived, you went to your work station and just picked up from where you left off the day before. Your friend asked if you wanted to go for lunch and you said you didn't know.

Understanding your attitude. If you are happy and optimistic all the time, that's wonderful. Many people wish they could be more like that. This might just be your nature, and that's great. Recognize that being overly happy or optimistic may not be realistic in a particular situation, so you should still develop an awareness of matching your mood to the circumstances.

If you tend to be negative and pessimistic, work to see where this attitude comes from. It might not be that you have poor emotional intelligence or a feeling of unwellness; it could just be that you have a bad habit. Was one of your parents like that? Have you always been that way? Do you just not really care how you come across to others? If you can see where the behavior originates, you might be better able to reverse it by breaking the bad habit.

Someone who is ambivalent may need something to get excited about. Is your life dull and boring? Do you need to set goals and have something to look forward to? Are you not being challenged at work? You might just be running on "auto-pilot" and have to do something a little differently to shake things up in your life.

Managing your attitude. You might not be able to change your natural response to things, but you can choose your attitude, which in turn will influence your responses. Work to recognize that you are defaulting to a certain attitude and choose a different one instead. Some people use appreciation journals to reflect on the things in their life they are grateful for. Others wake up every morning and choose to be happy and positive; though they sometimes forget that by the time they get to the office. Notice the effect that little things have on you throughout the day, and work to remind yourself about the attitude you chose when you began your day. A great motto is, "Don't worry about that which you cannot change." Also, don't allow others' negativity to become contagious; recognize when you are mirroring those around you.

Tanis is not a morning person, or so she says. She arrives at work grumpy and listless each day, and tells people not to bug her until she's had her coffee. It's usually around noon by the time Tanis shakes off her morning blues. By then, she has moved on to complaining about customers which dominates the lunch room conversation. Her behavior is similar in the afternoon, and includes her stressing out about all of the work she has to do. This continues until about five minutes to quitting time when Tanis gets her coat and prepares to rush out the door for the day. Yesterday, a big client called in a change to an order and Tanis completely freaked out. She couldn't believe the inconvenience the customer was causing her. She yelled out orders to all the floor staff, as they tried to avoid her.

Tanis does not seem to be aware of her attitude or how it might be affecting others in the workplace. If she were to change her morning routine, choose to be happy and positive at work, and then remind herself to continue that throughout the day, she might enjoy her day more and not feel the need to rush out the door. A positive attitude would also enable her to better handle stressful situations; she could be more resilient when emergencies come up.

List something you have done at work when you have had a negative attitude. _____

_____

How would things look differently in that situation if you were to have a positive attitude? _____

_____

Now, try out a positive attitude for the day instead. Write down the things you are going to do to achieve this. _____

_____

_____

List the ways your day was impacted by having a positive attitude. _____

_____

_____

Build your MeYouQ by consciously choosing your attitude and being mindful of maintaining that attitude throughout the day.

Chapter 11 Takeaways:

↗ Your attitude affects your level of enjoyment, and determines how you will relate to others

↗ Your attitude attracts more of the same and is what you tend to notice and conclude about people and situations

↗ You can choose your attitude and should be aware of which attitude you are defaulting to throughout the day

↗ It takes work to recognize and modify your attitude, but it can be done by being appreciative and consciously eliminating the negativity in your life

↗ A positive attitude will increase your resilience and reduce the stress brought on by problem situations

Stress and unhappiness may not originate from your attitude, but rather from the effect your personal standards have on the different areas of your life.

Chapter 12: Your Personal Standards

Are your expectations positively impacting your experiences?

PERSONAL STANDARDS ARE THE BEHAVIORS each of us believes should be exhibited in a variety of situations. They form the benchmark used to judge one's own behavior, and the behavior of those around them. A person's standards can change as they have new experiences and develop new beliefs.

The criteria for your goals are based on your standards, so if you have high personal standards, you have likely set higher goals and expectations for performance. If you have low personal standards, you are likely to set lower goals and expectations for performance. It's a self-fulfilling prophecy that you will only attempt to achieve what you expect from yourself; you will put in the corresponding amount of effort in pursuit of your goals.

Having and meeting high standards for your behavior will help you achieve more in life, but it can put excessive pressure on you as well. If you set unrealistic expectations for your behavior, or the behavior of others, you might find yourself disappointed often. It may be easier to set lower expectations, so you are more easily pleased; the risk is that you won't achieve your maximum potential operating that way. A balance is needed.

The idea is to set standards that drive you to achieve, but don't set you up for constant failure, or continually cause stress and disappointment. Goals should be challenging and attainable, and a few disappointments are ok.

Recognize that other people's behaviors result from their personal standards, which can be different than yours. This has the potential to cause conflict if you cannot agree on a performance standard or make a decision together. You may find yourself in a situation where you feel you need to compromise your standards, and you are unwilling to do so. Alternatively, trying to motivate someone to aspire to a higher standard, more in line with your own, can be frustrating.

Explore your personal standards now, and work from recognizing to understanding to management.

Recognizing your personal standards. What are the standards you set for your own behavior? Do you have a strong work ethic and prefer to have things done a certain way, or are you easygoing and unconcerned about it? Do you have certain expectations of how others should behave? For example, how a customer service representative should treat you?

Do you see yourself as an example of hard work and encourage others to reach higher standards? Are you someone who puts too much pressure on yourself to be perfect? Do you focus on the flaws or drawbacks in things and have a difficult time accepting them for what they are?

Are you easily persuaded to just accept sub-par performance? Do you find your standards sliding because of those around you?

Are you getting tired of asking for what you are not getting? Do you feel that everything is overpriced and that it is difficult to find value?

Your personal standards may be different in the various areas of your life. For instance, what are your expectations for items like food, clothing, home decor, and entertainment; do you care more about some things than others? Are you willing to let your expectations slide in certain areas of your life, while maintaining high expectations in others? Perhaps you have high standards at work, but are more relaxed at home.

Understanding your personal standards. Your level of expectations can cause you to be constantly disappointed or easily pleased. You might be annoyed by those around you when they don't have a strong work ethic or don't care about quality. Your particularness might be a good thing, as you refuse to settle for mediocre items and don't waste your money on junk, however it might be frustrating to others if you are never happy and are unreasonable.

How are your personal standards affecting what you are achieving in life? Are you dissatisfied, or settling for less than you should? When your standards are too high, you might be disappointed when people, situations, and events frequently don't live up to them. It may seem as though nothing is good enough. When your standards are too low, however, you might forfeit the nice things in life and quality output at work. You may not be having the best sensory experiences available in your environment, or may miss out on job opportunities given to those with outstanding performance.

If your personal standards are causing problems in different areas of your life, you can change your expectations, which in turn changes your outcomes.

Managing your personal standards. Becoming aware of the pressure you are, or are not, placing on yourself and others, can be important in setting and achieving goals and being able to work as part of a team. Awareness will also help you to recognize where your expectations may be too high, allowing you to adjust them to be more realistic for the situation.

If you are constantly disappointed by unmet expectations, consider that your standards may be unreasonable. It's not that you need to have low standards, but thinking about your personal standards and managing your expectations might help ease some of the stress in your life.

If your expectations are "reasonable," you may need to persuade others to see your point of view so you can get the results you want. Perhaps you will be able to convince some people and not others. All you can do is try, and realize that you cannot control everything in life.

If nothing great is happening in your life, you might consider whether your personal standards are at play. Use a different standard when making choices at home and at work, and see if positive changes happen.

Alexa earned a "meets expectations" rating on her last performance appraisal and she was quite pleased with herself. Because she is meeting expectations, she thought she would ask her boss for a raise. Her boss would like to see Alexa try harder before she gets a raise. Alexa can't understand why she needs to work harder when she is already meeting expectations.

Alexa may not ever get her raise or be eligible for a promotion if she doesn't set a higher standard for her behavior and motivate herself to higher performance. Her future could be limited if she is always waiting for someone else to motivate her.

Jill is a perfectionist. She puts a lot of pressure on herself to do her work exceptionally well, and in doing so is often redoing work that other people have submitted. Jill resents that she is the only one in the workplace who does a good job and that she ends up doing all the work. She thinks her workplace is full of incompetent people.

Jill is going to burnout if she can't manage her expectations, or end up furious with her co-workers if she can't persuade them to see things differently. She might need to scale back her expectations, or convince her boss and co-workers to increase theirs. She needs to remind herself that it is ok to have challenging expectations and high standards if they are attainable and realistic. If things are not going to change, she might need a new work environment where people have a similar work ethic to hers.

What is the last goal you set for yourself? _____

_____

What standard of performance are you expecting from yourself to achieve your goal? _____

_____

Is this an appropriate expectation for your performance? Are you pushing yourself too hard, or not hard enough? If so, what might a better personal standard be in this situation? _____

_____

_____

Build your MeYouQ by working to develop reasonable expectations in the different areas of your life.

Chapter 12 Takeaways:

↗ A source of your frustration in life and with others could be your personal standards

↗ Recognize you might be judging people and outcomes unfairly because of your own personal standards being too high

↗ Conflict can arise when one person isn't living up to the other person's standards; you may have to lower your standards or work harder to meet theirs

↗ Having high standards can lead to the finer things in life and drive people to success, but if you are never satisfied you could become frustrated; alternatively, if your standards are too low, you may be settling for less than what you could achieve

Personal standards was the last area of the SELF. Read on to reflect on what was covered in this section.

Wrapping Up You as a SELF

IN THIS SECTION OF PART 1, you examined the personal behaviors that need to be managed before you can build effective relationships with other people. The major themes covered were:

Personality. People have different tendencies and strengths because of their personality types. These include: whether or not they become energized by being around others, keeping their options open and postponing a decision as long as possible, consulting others when making a decision, and thinking abstractly and creatively. Recognize the effect each dimension of personality may have on a situation and work to balance it with attention to the opposite side of that dimension. For example, if you are too introverted, you can push yourself to be more outgoing when a situation calls for it.

Emotions. Your emotions can creep up on you and cause you to react in a negative way. If you can recognize an emotion as it is beginning to cause a reaction, you can control the reaction and choose a more appropriate response. When you can do this for yourself, you can assist others in managing their emotions as well. For example, when you are angry with someone, you might be inclined to yell at him, but you can stop yourself and choose to have a calm conversation with him instead.

Self-esteem. Healthy self-esteem can give you confidence, but it must come from inside you. You need to evaluate your self-esteem and see if it is holding you back or causing others to be annoyed with you. If your self-esteem is low, practice taking credit for the things you do well and not being too hard on yourself for mistakes you make. For example, if you don't feel you deserve a raise, you will never ask for one and never receive one. If your self-esteem is too high, you need to be realistic about your abilities or you may find yourself in a situation where you cannot perform as well as you think. For example, you think anyone can build a garage, so you work on the project but find out later that you made several mistakes because you didn't know what you didn't know.

Creativity. Your creativity can be used to make things better, which is sometimes good and sometimes not so good. Depending on the situation, you may have to reign in your creativity because it is unnecessarily causing extra work or negative emotions. Creativity can be good, but it needs to be channeled in the right way and even turned off sometimes. For example, if you find you cannot work within an existing system because you are constantly searching for ways to improve it, you are going to frustrate yourself if you have no power to make the changes. You should learn to accept that which you cannot change.

Anxiety proneness. Too much anxiety can prevent you from taking chances and seizing opportunities in your life. You need to recognize when you are holding yourself back with unnecessary worry, and work to push yourself in the right direction. Adopt a more appropriate view of the situation, and take small steps toward doing whatever it is you are afraid to do. For example, you might really want to switch careers and do what you love, but the unknown is far too scary. Perhaps with careful planning you can eventually make the move happen.

Values. Your values are relatively unchanging and define what you feel is important in life, what you aspire to. If you can identify your personal values, you can make choices that are in line with what will make you happy and fulfilled in life. You will experience discomfort when you do things that go against your values if you aren't choosing properly. Find situations that are going to help you fulfill one or more of your values. For example, if you value helping others, you might have a hard time with quotas at work that say you have to serve a certain number of customers every hour, because they mean you have to sacrifice the personal attention you enjoy giving people. Perhaps another workplace has the structure you need.

Needs. Your needs drive your behavior and are changing all the time. When one need is fulfilled, another one is there to take its place. If you can be aware of your needs at any given time, you can choose actions that will lead to a feeling of fulfillment. If you can't fulfill your needs, you will be left with a wanting feeling. For example, if you have the need to feel accepted, you require people to tell you that you are important and valued; an increase in pay isn't likely to fill the need. Seek out a situation where you are given acknowledgement and appreciation in one way or another. The idea is to choose a positive, productive way to fill the need.

Spirituality. When you live in regret of the past, or worry about the future, you are not living life in the present. You can't change the past but you can learn from it; you can't control the future but you can plan for it, so living in the moment is the only thing that can bring your spirit peace. Believing you are connected to something bigger than you can be a comforting feeling. For example, if you are always worried about how you are measuring up to the standards of others, instead of appreciating yourself for the being that was put on this earth for a reason, you can never be at peace with yourself.

Feeling of wellness. Some days you may feel as if you are not yourself, but you don't know why. If you can look at your level of wellness in the different areas of your life, for instance, finances, relationships, health, or community, you may discover the root cause of these feelings; then you are able to work on a solution to the problem. Without this perspective, you may not know which problem to work on. For example, your friends are always bugging you to go out and you just don't have time for them. Each time they ask, it stresses you out, and you wonder why they have to get together so often anyway—you're too busy for that. However, when they go without you, you feel disappointed and left out. These feelings may be telling you that you need to make time for your friends because you do miss them and need them in your life.

Previous experiences. You have had a unique upbringing with different people and life experiences. Your past experiences have impressed habits and beliefs on you that affect your thoughts, choices, and behavior today. Be aware of how you may or may not be thinking or acting appropriately in your new experiences, and work to develop new thoughts or behaviors. For example, when you recognize that the atmosphere of teasing and sarcasm that you grew up in may not be appropriate in your business environment, you will be conscious about what you say to people and avoid these behaviors.

Attitude. Your optimism or pessimism may need to be put aside for a more realistic point of view in some situations, though a positive outlook is generally preferred. Ambivalence could perhaps be turned into caring more about the perceptions of others. Choosing your attitude consciously will allow you to live each day positively and to its full potential, although you may have to remind yourself throughout the day to maintain that attitude. For example, you wake up in the morning and decide that you are not going to let anything bother you today. Then you get to work, where you have a negative boss who could ruin your work day. You will need to choose to see the positive side of things and enjoy your day, in spite of your boss's attitude.

Personal standards. The expectations you have for your own behavior can be motivating and result in you getting ahead and having the things you want in life. Your expectations can also cause frustration if you feel you are the only one who cares or works hard, or if you are never satisfied with the products and services available. Awareness about your personal standards can show you where your expectations are serving you and where they might need to be adjusted to serve you better. For example, if you can't seem to get ahead at the office, you might need to set higher standards to work towards. Aim for *excellent* instead of *meets expectations*.

You may discover additional characteristics about yourself which have not been covered. Give these the same attention in terms of recognizing, understanding, and management. Work to foster a more objective, realistic view, but don't be afraid to challenge yourself to grow and develop. Become aware and remain aware.

Once you are able to do this for yourself, you will notice these things in other people. You might ask people more about their strengths, emotions, self-esteem, creativity, anxiety levels, values, needs, spirituality, wellness, experiences, attitudes, and personal standards. As you get to know yourself better you can get to know others better, what makes them who they are and why they do what they do.

MeYouQ in Action

Stella gets upset with the noise level and all the visiting that goes on in the office; she can "never get any work done." She is an above average performer, gets along with others, and has good attendance at work; but lately she is unhappy with her job and thinks about looking for a new one.

Stella decides to talk to her boss about the disruptions in the office. The boss doesn't see the problem and is quite happy with everyone's level of productivity. He tells Stella that she has been a valued employee for the last 10 years, but he is sorry he can't do anything to address her concerns. As Stella just learned about the concept of *MeYouQ*, she begins to wonder if the problem isn't the situation; it might be in her thinking.

Stella would like to build her *MeYouQ* because she read that it is the key to having more inner peace and building strong relationships with others, both of which she would like to achieve. She decides to start looking at the various aspects of her SELF.

Thinking about the type of person Stella appears to be, go through the questions below and write out some things she could discover about her SELF. When you are done, read on further to see some suggested answers.

Which of Stella's traits might be at play in this situation?

- ☐ Personality
- ☐ Emotions
- ☐ Self-esteem
- ☐ Creativity
- ☐ Anxiety Proneness
- ☐ Values
- ☐ Needs
- ☐ Spirituality
- ☐ Feeling of Unwellness
- ☐ Previous Experience
- ☐ Attitude
- ☐ Personal Standards

In what ways can this mindfulness give her a sense of peace with who she is? _____

_____

_____

_____

_____

What options, other than quitting her job, does she have now?

_____

_____

_____

When Stella is struggling with something like she is in this case, she can examine the role she could be playing in the situation. She might analyze her own behavior this way:

"Why am I feeling like I want to quit my job? Is the noise that bad? Why can't I get over it? Is it just my personality, and the fact that I am more on the introverted side, that all the socializing bothers me? Am I having a hard time managing my emotions and am I getting myself worked up about nothing? Is my self-esteem at play and I think people should be more like me? Maybe I value hard work and doing a good job, and others don't have these same values. Or perhaps it isn't even the noise bothering me. Maybe I am looking for an excuse to quit my job because I don't feel like my needs are being fulfilled here. If I was more spiritual, maybe I could stop my mind from racing and telling me to quit. Perhaps my financial or family problems are causing me to feel unwell, and the real problem isn't even at work. Maybe the way I grew up, which was quiet without a lot of communication, is the way I expect things to be today. Maybe I am just in a bad mood and I need to choose a positive attitude when I come to work. Or perhaps I just have certain standards for behavior at work that other people don't possess."

These types of questions will help Stella to narrow down the potential source of her thinking and be mindful about her situation. She will be able to choose the most suitable behavior in light of this new awareness. She may see that she doesn't have to quit her job, but could change her thinking instead, or choose a course of action to deal with an underlying problem in her life.

You can look at your own situations in a similar manner. When you can see why you do what you do, you can work to consciously choose your behavior. You will feel less torn or confused and more in control of your thoughts and actions.

To become better at pinpointing the source of your behavior, you need to know yourself better. Gain a little more practice in building your self-awareness by thinking about all of the traits you just discovered. Begin to know yourself better by answering the following questions:

List one of your specific traits that you think might need some work. _____

Explain how this trait could cause a problem for you. _____

_____

_____

Explain how this trait can be used in a positive way. _____

_____

_____

List another one of your specific traits that you can work on. ____

_____

Explain how this trait could cause a problem for you. _____

_____

_____

Explain how this trait can be used in a positive way. _____

_____

_____

Continue to explore your traits and the things you do until you have a really good sense of awareness and are regularly mindful about them. Work to choose the most appropriate action as much as possible.

In all of this, learn to love and understand yourself as a unique individual. Don't be so critical of yourself or wish you were someone different. Take control over your life, set goals, and a find a sense of purpose that is congruent with who you are.

Make conscious choices about the tasks and roles you take on, so you can achieve peace and accomplish other goals in your life.

Recognize your inner voice, the ego, when it's working against you, and when you are feeling stressed out. Live in the present, while learning your lessons from the past and planning for multiple possible futures. Stay mindful of your other characteristics as well. Determine which traits trigger certain behaviors, and be conscious in choosing your actions.

The characteristics covered in this section were your internal ones, your SELF. Move on to building your *MeYouQ* further by examining what you are like around your peers; you as an OTHER. This will show you additional behaviors that must be managed. The strategy is a bit different, in addition to self-reflection, you will gain the perspective of another person.

Section 2: You as an OTHER

Do others see you the way you would like them to?

IN YOUR RELATIONSHIPS WITH OTHERS, you have actions, interactions, and different points of view. The effectiveness of these relationships is determined by how well you work to manage the impressions other people have of you (Chapter 13), the manners you use (Chapter 14), your communication style (Chapter 15), and the things you do to relate to others (Chapter 16). How you interact and how successful your interactions are will be influenced by things like your approachability, sense of humor, open-mindedness, assertiveness, interest in others, and cooperativeness.

Because the attributes discussed in this section are only observable around other people, you can't count on self-assessment to be enough. Your development in this section is going to involve getting feedback from others; think about a person in your life that you can trust with this important task, someone who will be candid.

One of the most difficult things you can do is to ask someone to be completely honest with you and then listen to them without getting defensive. As difficult as this is, if you can't get honest feedback about your behavior, you may never know what aspects need improvement. Please keep an open mind as you work through this section. The assumptions you are making about yourself may be flawed by being either too critical or not critical enough, and you may have to push yourself to trust others in your personal development. Continue your journey or personal development now with Impression Management.

You as an Other Takeaways:

↗ *MeYouQ* will help you influence others and build relationships

↗ It is important to get a sense of how others see you, and you do this by asking someone you trust as a good judge of the behavior

---

Chapter 13: Impression Management

What do you do to influence how others see you?

WHETHER YOU REALIZE IT OR NOT, you work to present yourself to others in a certain way in an effort to have them form a favorable impression of you and be attracted to you for different reasons. You do this by controlling what you say and what aspects of yourself you allow others to see. You end up with a certain demeanor that others will use to form an opinion of you and, ultimately, to judge you.

Some people don't care what others think of them. This just isn't a useful point of view for someone who wants to get ahead in life. People are expected to work with and cooperate with others to achieve many things. If a person can get others to think favorably about him, he is more likely to be extended opportunities, or be recommended by them. If a person doesn't care whether people like him in his personal life, perhaps he can separate that and at least practice impression management for the workplace. That's a start, anyway.

Before you examine the impression management strategies you are currently using, look at some general qualities that can attract others to you and cause them to admire you. You will also see how you can build these qualities: professionalism, confidence, capability, approachability, being political, and leadership.

Professionalism. Behaving in a professional manner involves meeting the standard expected for people doing a certain job. People act in a certain way in order to be viewed as trustworthy in their area of practice. They dress a certain way, say the right things, exhibit the correct behaviors, and possess the required knowledge. Until they can play the role expected of them on a subconscious level, they have to consciously be aware of every move they make.

The level and type of professionalism required will be different in different situations. When people aren't aware of the behavior expected, they can make mistakes and be seen as unprofessional. People need to ascertain the behavior requirements for different situations they may find themselves in and adjust their behavior accordingly. If they don't anticipate others' expectations, they may not be viewed the way they want to be. If they are coming across as awkward, goofy, or boisterous, for example, they need to practice better impression management. They can do this only by learning to take cues from others.

Confidence. For people to be trusted in their ability at work, they need to show others they are confident. If they appear to be unsure of their abilities, others will be unsure as well. In addition, people need to be able to show their confidence to others without coming across as being arrogant.

Confidence is shown by individuals who are able to talk about their abilities in a realistic way; of course they need self-esteem to do this. Confidence comes from being proud of achievements and knowing that future goals can be achieved as well. Being confident means that people know they can make mistakes, fix them and still be successful; it doesn't mean that a person is perfect.

A confident person can be honest about his abilities and give himself proper credit, without diminishing his achievements. A confident person is able to state his qualifications in an appropriate way, rather than bragging about his accomplishments and presenting himself as better than everyone else.

Being overconfident means a person does not have the skills and abilities she thinks she has. When a person represents her abilities to others, she needs to set herself in an appropriate light, so others can develop realistic expectations for her behavior and not be disappointed because she can't do what she said she could.

Capability. Being capable is related to being professional and having confidence, but it is more about demonstrating the behavior and not about appearances. When a person is working within his scope of ability and meeting organizational goals, he is showing he is capable.

A person will find it difficult to show he is capable if he takes on work he is not qualified to do. Individuals need to be careful when they claim to have an ability, so they don't take on work they are unable to complete.

On the other hand, if a person is confident that she can learn and be successful, there might be nothing wrong with stretching her view of what she's capable of. Many people accept a new job and then worry they are in over their heads, but it works out just fine as they take it step by step. When a person represents herself to others, it can be dangerous to under- or overestimate her actual capabilities. In either case, it can affect her ability to grow, develop, and be successful.

Approachability. Being seen as approachable might be useful for impression management, especially if a person is working closely with others. It is important to come across as being open to listening to new ideas and information, even if a person doesn't really feel that way.

If someone is unhappy and stressed all the time, his co-workers won't be comfortable approaching him with important details that could impact the success of the whole team. If people don't approach him because they are afraid of how he will respond, they might not get the support they need from him.

Impression management in this area means that a person appears approachable even if he is feeling unhappy or stressed. He can do this by making sure he doesn't get upset with employees when they come to him; he gives them his time and attention, and practices good listening skills.

Being Political. Engaging in politics at work carries a negative connotation these days. It can mean that a person is willing to hurt or use others in an effort to advance his own interests. Playing politics means a person forms relationships with the goal of gaining something in the future.

While being political is generally seen as negative, it can be acceptable when a person is forming relationships for the benefit of everyone in the workplace. For example, when there are limited resources, and management has to choose where to focus, they may provide the support to the area where they like the supervisor the most.

A person may have to engage in politics to some extent to gain favors in the workplace; it seems to be human nature that people respond to schmoozing and ingratiation. Playing politics can be seen as necessary for the success of your organization or department, whether you like it or not.

Leadership. Some people lead and some people follow. If a person wants to be perceived as a leader, she has to demonstrate that she can do more than just follow. This does not mean arguing with the boss. Leaders have a vision and they are able to choose a course of action with confidence and accuracy. Leaders are able to articulate their vision to others and inspire them to follow along.

To be viewed as a leader, a person needs to take on leadership roles, formal or informal, and behave as a leader does. She will have to gain the trust of others, develop her vision, and inspire others to follow. She needs to be the type of person that others want to follow—this is *MeYouQ!* You will learn more about building your leadership skills in Chapter 23.

Think about a person who you see in a favorable light. What have they done to manage the impressions that others have about them? List the specific things they do, or how they come across, that lead you to see them in a positive light. _____

_____

_____

Are you conscious about your impression management efforts? Do you act like yourself around others or do you try to control what people see? List some ways you try to control what others see. _____

_____

_____

When you are meeting someone for the first time, what do you allow them to see? Are you careful with how you speak and what you say, or do you pay no special attention to what you are saying or doing? Can you read the situation and determine how you are coming across to the person? List some things people do to show approval or disapproval of your actions. _____

_____

_____

_____

_____

Have you consciously thought about how people see you at work each day, what they think of you and how they would describe you? Write down what you think others would say if they were asked to describe you in terms of being professional, confident, capable, approachable, political, and showing leadership.

_____

_____

_____

_____

_____

_____

_____

_____

_____

Gain feedback. You have arrived at the challenging part. Choose someone you trust at work who can give you honest feedback about how you are coming across to others, and ask him or her to describe you as if he or she was describing you to someone else. Ask specific questions to see if he or she sees you the way you are trying to portray yourself. For example, does this person see you as a leader or as showing confidence? Also, ask them what they think you can do to come across more effectively in terms of your goals.

> **Were you happy with the way your co-worker described you? Is that the way you want to be seen? If you want people to see you differently, how would you want them to see you?** _____
>
> _____
>
> _____
>
> **What things will you do to encourage people to see you this way?**
>
> _____
>
> _____
>
> _____
>
> _____
>
> _____

When you can recognize that some of your many traits might be operating automatically, and not in the most favorable way, you can choose the behavior that is right for the situation. Become aware and remain aware.

Use self-monitoring to see how you might be coming across to others. Look for cues that indicate whether your behavior is being viewed as acceptable or not. When you are unsure, ask people what the expected behavior is in different situations. Adjust your behavior as required to gain favorable reactions, and ask people you trust to give you honest feedback. For example, you might ask whether it would be appropriate to stay for a visit after giving a business presentation. If you are not sure and you can't ask someone, be mindful of whether others are engaging with you after the presentation, or if they are ignoring you. If they are distracted or uninterested, it is time to leave.

Build your MeYouQ by seeing yourself the way others see you and making adjustments to your behavior so people have favorable impressions of you.

Chapter 13 Takeaways:

↗ Impression management is your attempt to control what you reveal about yourself to others, so you can influence what they think of you

↗ You will need to do certain things to be seen as professional, confident, capable, approachable, political, and a leader

↗ Use self-monitoring and make adjustments to your behavior in the right way to successfully manage impressions made of you

Another way people form impressions about us is by observing the way we treat others. Read about manners and etiquette next.

Chapter 14: Your Manners

Are you following the rules of etiquette?

RULES OF ETIQUETTE DESCRIBE what is appropriate in different situations and in different companies. Are people expected to take turns, hold the door for others, keep elbows off the table during meals, replace the paper in the photocopier, or let the boss go first? These things are important for impression management, but they are also important for getting along with others. Sometimes people are not aware of the unwritten rules they should be following in business situations.

While there can be many different expectations for behavior, have a look at the following basic manners for the workplace in terms of helping others, cooperating, showing respect, being inclusive, and having patience.

Helping others. Some people just don't think to help others; they are not compelled to act or they don't realize a person is in need—maybe they don't care. When you are working with a group of people, it's nice to pitch in and not only do your fair share, but to put forth an extra effort to help your team.

Helping others doesn't mean that you must take on their work, but it can be nice to offer to help people when they need it, if you are able. If someone is struggling with jammed paper in the photocopier, you could offer to assist. If someone is being berated by a customer, you could step in and help diffuse the situation. We all have different strengths and weaknesses, so some people may not find certain things as easy to do as others will. It may not take much effort to lend a hand to someone who is struggling with a task you excel at.

When someone helps you out at work "pay it forward" and spread the spirit of helping others. It usually doesn't take much time or effort to make someone's day run more smoothly. What a wonderful way to build a community with those you work with and see every day!

Cooperating. When people cooperate with others, it means they play fair while working together to accomplish a common goal. They strive to make things easier for each other, not more difficult. To cooperate, means to get along with others, offer useful information, and put the collective need ahead of personal desires.

People who can't work collaboratively have no role in this world of teamwork. By using teams, organizations find that better decisions are made, and better products and services are generated than when individuals are working on their own.

Cooperation can also benefit individuals personally, for instance, involving others can help a person critique and expand his own ideas. When a person cooperates with others on a project and helps them achieve their goals, it can result in gaining support for what he wants at another time. It can be very difficult for him to meet his own goals if no one is helping him.

Showing respect. It is crucial to show respect for others. This means showing respect for them as human beings, for their ideas, for their efforts and struggles, and for their feelings. Respect means not talking behind people's backs or saying bad things about them. Respect also means allowing them to speak and not putting them down for what they say.

A person can show respect for others' personal space and privacy as well. Not all people want others to know about their personal lives, so it is important to keep private information confidential. Respect is treating people the way _they_ want to be treated.

Respect for authority is also important. A person who undermines his boss will not be looked upon favorably and may not be trusted by others. This means he should support his boss and not do anything to detract from his credibility. If he disagrees with the methods his boss is using, he should talk to him directly about it and not damage morale by spreading negative information around the workplace. When his boss asks him to do something, he should respect that authority and comply (as long as it's something the boss should be asking him to do, otherwise many organizations have whistleblower programs for these situations).

Being inclusive. Being inclusive means not leaving anyone out. When there are opportunities and events at work, everyone needs to be included. When people are being consulted, everyone needs to be included fairly, maybe not every time, but at least given an equal opportunity to be involved. When you are sharing non-confidential information about the organization, employees need to be included equally.

Being inclusive may not be normal for some people. In-groups and out-groups exist in many organizations, families, and societies. If these groups have formed in the workplace, people need to break down barriers and work towards inclusion by reaching out and encouraging others to be involved.

Inclusiveness and respect go hand in hand. When people exclude others at work, it is disrespectful. When some people are excluded, it seems like others are being favored with opportunity and knowledge. This is unfair, and a person who is engaging in this behavior might appear as though he is discriminating against certain individuals. Being inclusive creates a pleasant work atmosphere; people can go to work knowing they will be treated fairly. They can relax and do their jobs without distraction.

Having patience. It's inevitable that people at work are going to have questions, require information, and need support or assistance from each other. When dealing with others, it is important to recognize that not everyone works at, or learns at, the same pace. While this might require using up someone else's valuable time, it is important to provide good internal customer service to employees and help to ensure their workplace needs are met.

If you don't have the time to assist a co-worker without becoming impatient, ask to arrange a different time, or try to get someone else to provide assistance. Use your emotional intelligence to recognize when you are beginning to get impatient and choose an appropriate response instead. If people are asking questions that have already been answered, try to repeat the information without getting upset—many people don't pay attention to information until they need to use it.

A common reason someone might become impatient is that he is being interrupted too frequently. To manage these disruptions, he may have to set boundaries regarding what others can expect from him; such as, suggesting people wait to approach him until they have a list of questions, or asking not to be disturbed when his door is closed, unless it is an emergency. By controlling his response and setting boundaries, he will have the patience to help others when they need it.

Do you think you have good manners, or do you sometimes act in inappropriate ways? Think about the last time you were around others and had less than perfect manners. What happened? _____

_____

What should you have done in that situation instead? _____

_____

Think about a time when someone used bad manners with you. What happened? _____

_____

How did this make you feel? _____

What should he or she have done in that situation instead? _____

_____

Gain feedback. It's time to ask your trusted co-worker to provide an honest assessment of your manners. Tell him or her about the topics covered in this section, and ask whether you are guilty of any of these things. Listen with an open mind and see where you might be able to improve.

> **Write down some feedback you were given that you might be able to work on.** _____
>
> _____
>
> **Can you accept this feedback objectively and see room for improvement? What specifically are you going to do to improve?**
>
> _____
>
> _____
>
> _____

Build your MeYouQ by seeing the various opportunities to show good manners and by paying more attention to the little things you can do for others.

> **Chapter 14 Takeaways:**
> ↗ Helping others, cooperating, showing respect, being inclusive, and having patience are important for getting along with others
> ↗ Using good manners in the workplace can result in people being kind to you and helping you when you need it
> ↗ Manners are important for exercising good internal customer service and expressing yourself in an appropriate way

Getting along with others involves having good manners. Your communication skills will also help you show respect and inclusiveness to others.

Chapter 15: Your Communication Style

Are you having frequent miscommunications?

PEOPLE COMMUNICATE IN MANY different ways. A person's communication skills are formed based on their observations of others and their own trial and error. If a person is not able to have her needs met using one communication style, she will try something else. If a method works, it will be repeated. Sometimes the methods people use with others are not the most appropriate or effective, and the relationship can be affected.

Your ability to communicate effectively is important in order for you to work well with others. If you can avoid miscommunications in the workplace, you will have a more pleasant work atmosphere and increase your chances of having your own needs met. You will be able to ask for the resources you need to do your job and for growth opportunities. Good communication also means you are able to hold others accountable for what they are supposed to be doing at work, whether you are a boss or a team member.

In this chapter, you will discover some proven methods for communicating effectively in the workplace. Included in the discussion are the communication model, active listening, using "I" language, giving and accepting feedback, and conflict resolution.

Communication model. Perhaps you have seen this model before. It begins with the sender of a message having an idea he wants to share. He forms the idea and encodes the message in a way he hopes the receiver will understand. He sends the message through some sort of medium, like an e-mail or a phone call, and hopes it reaches the intended audience. The intended audience receives the message and decodes it while forming her own conclusions about what the message means. She acknowledges the message or asks for more information, or he checks to see that she understands the message, clarifies if she doesn't, and the communication loop is complete. Sounds simple in theory, but there can be problems at any point in the process.

When the sender is selecting the message to send, he may not realize that the message will be inappropriate for, or not applicable to, the receiver. When encoding the message, he might use language the receiver won't understand, or he might make assumptions about what the receiver already knows or doesn't know. When sending the message, his call might become disconnected or might choose an inappropriate medium. For example, if it's a private message and he uses a public medium, the receiver would get upset. When delivering the message, he might be in her personal space, talking too close, or she may not be paying attention to what he is saying. He might use body language that conflicts with the message. For example, he might be delivering good news with a worried look on his face. Depending on the culture he grew up in, he might use a tone of voice that she won't appreciate if she is not from that culture.

When the recipient then receives the message and is working to interpret it, she may read things into it that aren't there. She might not pick up on sarcasm or humor and take things too seriously. She might have interrupted him and not received the full message. Her own biases and expectations may interfere with the intended message if she doesn't pay attention to the details, or she jumps to conclusions too quickly. In the end, she might interpret a different message than the one that was intended. If the sender doesn't check with the receiver to see if she understood the message correctly, or if the receiver makes assumptions about what is being said, they will have a miscommunication.

When you use the communication process, how attentive are you to the different parts? Do you think about only sending messages that are appropriate for the intended audience? Do you just send out, or say whatever comes to mind? Do you think about how to word the message so the receiver will understand it, based on his experiences and knowledge? Do you stop to think about how your biases could affect the message you send? Are you considerate of the receiver's emotions about the message? Do you ensure your writing makes sense and your spelling is correct? Do you select an appropriate medium? When a personal touch is required, for example, do you pick up the phone instead of sending a text or email?

When you are on the receiving end of the message, do you ensure that you have received the full message before reacting to it? Do you work to ensure that your own biases are not clouding how you interpret the message? Do you think about the message and the intent of the sender before responding to the message? Do you take measures to make sure you have understood the message correctly, and ask for clarification when needed?

Good communication is the responsibility of both parties, just as a miscommunication is the fault of both parties. Ensuring appropriateness and understanding is a shared duty.

Think about the last time you were involved in a miscommunication where you were the one sending the message. What responsibility can you claim? _____

_____

What can you do better next time to ensure good communication?

_____

_____

_____

Active listening. Part of communicating well is being engaged with the speaker. When someone is talking to you, you should give her your undivided attention. If you are unable to do that, then maybe you need to postpone the conversation to a time when you can. Paying attention also means that you are not thinking about what you are going to say next, but you are actually listening to what is being said.

A person may not know whether or not you are paying attention or are engaged in the conversation. Active listening means having eye contact (in many cultures), nodding that you understand, paraphrasing what has been said to show that you understand, and asking questions for clarification. This way you won't be accused of not having listened to someone when they spoke to you; you will actually remember what they said.

Finally, active listening does not mean finishing people's sentences. Even if you think you know what she is going to say next, you should control yourself and not say it for her. Finishing a person's sentences can be very distracting and may cause her to lose her train of thought. Think about it this way, if you are talking, you are not listening.

Are you distracted when someone is talking to you? What kinds of distractions do you deal with? _____

_____

Think about a time you weren't listening as well as you could have been, and you ended up having a conflict with the other person. What could you have done to be a better listener? _____

_____

_____

"I" language. Using "I" language instead of "you" language is a powerful way to voice your concerns and wishes without sounding like you are blaming the other person. See the difference between the following two statements:

"You never clean up after yourself. I always have to do everything around here."

"I need help around here. Can I count on you to clean up after yourself?"

In the first example, the person may argue with you and insist he always cleans up. Using words like "never" and "always" don't help the situation either. It's likely that the person has cleaned up

131

before, it's not always you. If you use "you" language, you might find yourself in a no-win situation; you end up in conflict instead of gaining cooperation.

In the second example, you are able to state your needs without making the other person feel attacked. While it is often said that you can't "make" someone feel a certain way, many people are not self-aware enough to choose how they are going to react. In the second part of the sentence, the speaker asks a question to gain cooperation. Instead of stating what a person does or does not do, simply tell them what you would like them to do and ask if they will. You might also want to get them to commit to a timeline for action.

Using "I" language is part of being assertive. Assertiveness means being able to speak up for yourself in an appropriate way, without overstepping boundaries or infringing on the rights of others. Asserting yourself this way does not necessarily mean you will get what you want, but you increase your chances while keeping relationships intact. Being assertive does not mean that you always speak up for yourself, however; you may decide that it is inappropriate in a particular situation.

People who are not assertive engage in one or more of these other behaviors: passiveness, aggressiveness, or passive-aggressiveness.

Passive behavior results in the inability to speak up for oneself at all. A person who exhibits passive behavior often doesn't have his needs met. He won't say what he wants, and he will just let the other person decide. This is frustrating for both parties, the person who is not getting his needs met, and the person who always has to make the decisions. People who can't speak up for themselves also end up doing things they don't want to do because they don't know how to say, "No."

Aggressive behavior occurs when a person forces his views on someone else by using bullying behavior to achieve results. While the person using aggressive behavior may get what he wants, bullying people to gain their cooperation is not a good strategy for building relationships—it breaks them down instead. You might recognize an aggressive person through his use of a loud voice or threatening language; you will also notice the other person feels intimidated. The sad thing is this behavior works to get the bully the results he wants, so he keeps using it.

People with passive-aggressive behavior start out being passive and become aggressive when they don't get what they want. A person who is being passive-aggressive will begin feeling sorry for herself. She may say something like, "Nobody cares about me," or, "I never get to choose," then the behavior turns aggressive as she tries to make the other person feel bad. She may say something like, "You better help me or I'm going to make your life miserable," or, "Your needs are always more important than mine, aren't they? You are so selfish." You can see how this behavior might make someone appear a little "unstable." Being passive-aggressive is not a good strategy for someone who is trying to build relationships. Some people refer to this behavior as manipulative, and a person engaging in this type of conduct will not be trusted or respected.

You can see how assertive behavior is preferred. To become more assertive, begin to notice how you are wording things when you make requests of others. Catch yourself using the less desirable behaviors, and switch the wording to "I" language. Avoid using "guilt trips," where you try to make people feel guilty to achieve results. You should be able to get most of what you want by building relationships and using appropriate language, but remember that you won't get everything you want all the time, compromise may be required.

Write out a sentence that shows each of the different behaviors for the following scenario: You are the one who always has to stay late at work to help customers because you have no kids.

Passive response: _____

_____

Aggressive response: _____

_____

Passive-aggressive response: _____

_____

Assertive response: _____

_____

Now check these sample responses:

> *Passive: (thinks to himself, but can't speak up for himself, so he continues to stay late) "I wish I didn't have to stay late all the time, it's not fair."*

> *Aggressive: "I am sick and tired of all of you taking advantage of me! Someone else better stay or I'm going to lose it!"*

134

Passive-aggressive: (says) "No I don't mind staying late," (then thinks) "I'm going to get even with these people for taking advantage of me."

Assertive: "Excuse me everyone, I would like to talk to you about something. I have been the only one staying late with customers, and I think it's unfair. I would like to draw up a schedule so that we can all take turns."

Wouldn't it be great if everyone could communicate that well and work to have our needs met more often!

What is something you've wanted to say to someone but haven't? Write out how you can be assertive in this situation. _____

_____

_____

Gain feedback. Run through the statement above with your trusted co-worker. What do they think of phrasing things this way? Do they think you'll be successful?

Now try it out. How did it work? Were you successful? What would you do differently? _____

_____

If that was successful try again in another situation. Develop your technique until it works for you consistently.

Giving and receiving feedback. Are you able to give and receive feedback effectively? Giving feedback is important when you live and work with others. You want to be encouraging, and you also want to make sure people are learning and needs are being met. Giving feedback as a supervisor may be different than giving it as a peer, because people may feel they have to listen to the supervisor, but not to anyone else. In any case, you should be prepared to give both positive and corrective feedback to the people you work with.

When something is being done well you should let people know. Positive feedback is very motivating! It is demoralizing to hear only about the things you are doing poorly, so as much as possible, you should focus on the positive. Complimenting others doesn't come naturally to everyone; this could be something you will need to work on. Many people speak up only when they see something that needs improvement. This might be related to their previous experiences or attitudes they have.

When negative feedback must be given, you may want to take an approach to correct the behavior instead of just labeling it as "bad." Skills in assertiveness are needed to be able to give corrective feedback well. Instead of labeling someone's personality, you need to give specific feedback on the behavior you see, and explain what you would rather see instead. "You just seem lazy," becomes, "I notice that when there are slow times you don't look around for extra tasks to accomplish. I would like you to use your downtime to fill the containers, clean the washrooms, and restock the main fridge. Would you be able to take care of those things for me?" The first way of giving feedback—calling someone lazy—is likely to cause an argument, and the second is likely to change behavior. When you catch the employee doing good things, let her know, "The washrooms look great today! Thank you for taking care of that." Behavior that receives positive feedback will be repeated.

Being open-minded about input from others is another great quality to have, but it's not an easy thing to do. Recognize that other people may not focus on the positive and they might not have strong assertiveness skills, therefore, you may receive a negative message that sounds like blame. Instead of getting defensive or feeling demoralized, you can work to appreciate the message they are trying to give you. Ask for specific examples of the behavior they are talking about, and make an effort to understand what they are trying to say. Remember that people have their own opinions, and you might not agree with the feedback, but their comments may also really help you. Keep an open mind. If someone is negative all the time, ask them to also let you know when you are doing the right thing. Let them know that it is disheartening to receive only negative feedback, and you would appreciate knowing where you stand with all of your responsibilities.

When was the last time you gave positive feedback to someone? Is it time now? What will you say? _____

_____

Is there negative feedback you need to give someone, but you aren't sure what to say? Use your assertiveness skills and write out how to say it in a <u>corrective</u> (not negative) way. _____

_____

_____

Gain feedback. Run your idea by your trusted colleague, then try out the plan you created.

How was the positive feedback received? Did the person feel great? How did the corrective feedback work? How did the person respond? _____

_____

_____

What would you do differently next time? _____

_____

Conflict resolution. When you have conflict in your life, do you bottle it up, or are you able to address it with those involved? Your skills in assertiveness will help you to resolve conflict, but there's more to conflict resolution than being assertive; it takes cooperation as well.

Resolving conflict also means realizing that your view of reality is likely different from that of the other person. It would be a waste of time to try to get someone to agree that your view of reality is right; instead, you need to approach the situation from his view of reality. It doesn't matter what you think he did, it matters what he thinks he did. It may not matter what the situation was actually about, it may only matter what he thinks it was about. Work to understand a person's view fully. Consider this example of two people who disliked their meal at the same restaurant: One person says, "I hated my meal, this restaurant is horrible," while the other person says, "I didn't like the food I ordered, next time I'll try a different meal." A person's view becomes his truth.

When you have conflict with someone, you don't always need to be assertive and speak up for what you want. In cases where you fear violence or you know the person isn't going to see your side of the situation, you might want to just avoid the conflict entirely. If you are **avoiding** the situation, you aren't cooperating with the person either, but perhaps that's what the situation calls for. An example of where it is important to avoid conflict would be walking away from someone who is trying to attack or blame you for something. It's a no-win situation, so why bother?

Another instance when you wouldn't need to be assertive, but you would want to be cooperative, is a situation in which you want to let the other person have his way. Sometimes it's better to be **accommodating** and let the other person "win" because it's more important to him, or you would like to save your "win" for a time when the issue is very important to you. For example, if your co-worker wants to choose his vacation week first because he has a wedding to go to and your schedule is flexible, you may choose to accommodate that request.

An appropriate time to be assertive and not feel that you have to cooperate is one where you know you are the expert in the situation and you shouldn't compromise what you believe in. You choose to compete for your position or force your views on others because it's the right decision to make. This doesn't sound like cooperation, but that's ok in this situation. An example of when you might be **competing** with another person and demand to get your way is a situation where you have done thorough research in a certain area, and you know that to make any other choice would be costly.

Sometimes your argument has merit, but so does the other person's. This is often the case in the workplace today, and it results in both parties having to compromise to make the decision. By **compromising,** each person is being somewhat assertive and somewhat cooperative, and each still receives something in the outcome, although maybe not everything he or she had hoped for. An example of when to use compromise is a situation where your boss wants you to sell an extra 100 units, but you wanted to set the sales goal at 50 more units. The two of you might decide to set the goal at 75 units instead; no one got exactly what they wanted, but you both still received something.

Finally, the best result is a win-win scenario, where both parties cooperate and everyone gets exactly what they want. This type of an outcome takes collaboration, and **collaborating** takes time. While a win-win outcome is ideal, people don't always have the time to dedicate to figuring out the solution, and not every situation is so important that both parties need to receive everything they are asking for. An example of where a win-win outcome might be important is the sale of a business. Everyone wants to feel they were treated fairly and received what they wanted. One party got a price in the range she wanted, and the other party got support for a few weeks of transitioning into the business, for example.

Have you used these methods to handle conflict in your life? Some people are always competing for what they want, and they don't realize that sometimes the other person has to get what she wants too. When you work with others you need to be reasonable and decide what the best outcome is for the particular situation. However, it is important to recognize that you don't always have to cooperate with people who are being unreasonable.

Think about the last time you had conflict with someone and you feel as though you handled it poorly. Which style of conflict resolution did you use? (Hint: these are the words in bold above.) _____

How was your relationship with the person affected by this process? _____

What would have been a better way to deal with this situation?

_____

_____

Gain feedback. Ask your trusted co-worker if they feel you handle conflict effectively. Ask for any insight he or she can give you. Maybe you shy away from conflict when you should address it. Maybe the problem is that you aren't able to be assertive, or that all too often you compete for what you want at the expense of your relationships. Sounds like material for a great discussion over coffee!

> **Did you learn anything about your conflict handling style that you didn't know? How are you going to use this information to improve the way you handle conflict in the future?** _____
>
> _____
>
> _____

Your communication style will become extremely important as you begin to learn more about other people and build positive relationships with them. Continue to be conscious of your words and actions and make necessary adjustments.

Build your MeYouQ by examining the way you communicate, including choosing proper language, listening objectively, and caring about others.

Chapter 15 Takeaways:

↗ Good communication is important for the work atmosphere and for having your needs met

↗ Use the communication model to help you think about how you are sending messages and to ensure messages are getting to the recipient as intended

↗ Good communication requires giving the speaker your undivided attention and ensuring you understand what that person is saying

↗ Using "I" language is a non-threatening, respectful way to speak up for your needs

↗ Positive, corrective feedback should replace negative feedback; ensure you speak about the behavior and don't label the person. Be specific about the behaviors you want to see; people can't guess

↗ Listen to feedback objectively

↗ Assertiveness and cooperativeness will help you resolve conflict; work to see things from the other person's view of reality and realize sometimes the other person needs to "win"

Communication rounds out the information on *You as an OTHER*. Reflect on what you learned as you work through the next section.

Wrapping Up You as an OTHER

IN THIS SECTION OF PART 1, you examined personal behaviors that need to be managed before you can think about managing those of other people. The major themes covered were:

Impression management. You learned to self-monitor in different situations, so you can present yourself in such a way that people will form a favorable opinion of you. For example, you can determine the level of **professionalism** required, and adjust your behavior to suit the situation.

You recognize that you do not have to be perfect to be **confident**. You know not to brag and realize that being silent about your great abilities is not helpful either. Not only should you feel **capable**, you can demonstrate your capability by successfully completing the tasks you have taken on. Stretch yourself to accomplish more than before, but use caution.

Remember also to be open-minded and **approachable**. People should not be afraid to come to you when they need your help or advice. You recognize that you may need to play **politics** to help your department or team get the resources it needs to be successful. Don't be afraid to form relationships with those in power, but consider that it should not be for personal benefit.

You will continually work on your **leadership** skills, so people will want to follow you. Take cues from your employees on what is working and whether they are embracing the vision.

Your manners. Next you considered the effect your manners have on how you are seen by others. When building relationships you can forgive people who may not meet expectations for **etiquette**, as each person has strengths and weaknesses; however, you should do everything possible to ensure your own behavior is appropriate for the situation.

You are aware of how important it is to reach out and **help** others where possible. You recognize that a little bit of your time can mean a lot to a person, and your employees will need this attention. In addition, ensuring you play fair and **cooperate** with others will show your *MeYouQ*; you recognize opportunities for doing things right and better.

All human beings deserve a basic level of **respect**. You know not to speak badly of others, respecting each person and their right to privacy. You realize the importance of being **inclusive** at work as you provide opportunities equally to employees. You will no longer tolerate exclusion by others.

You will catch yourself becoming annoyed and choose to be **patient** with those who don't find tasks as easy as you do. You remember that each person is a unique individual with their own strengths, and that you can set boundaries for how you want to be treated.

Your communication style. As part of the **communication model**, you learned your part in conveying messages so they will be interpreted correctly by your audience. You recognize that miscommunication occurs when people don't take the time to ensure understanding. You practiced listening actively to ensure a person feels they have been heard and interpreted correctly. **Active listening** also helps people feel respected.

You were reminded to use **"I" language** because people feel blamed when "you" language is used. You can speak up for your needs and avoid creating, or exacerbating, a tense situation through the use of "I" language.

When giving feedback, you used **positive, corrective** language. This type of language encourages employees and maintains good relationships. Even if others don't give you feedback this way, you are able to be open-minded and look for aspects of truth in their messages.

Finally, you learned about **conflict resolution** and how you can make a choice on which style to use for the situation. Sometimes you will allow the other person to "win," so you can win next time. You learned that it takes time and energy to reach an agreement where everyone wins, so we often have to compromise.

MeYouQ in Action

Andy is trying to get a promotion at work, and he is focused on networking with members of the management team. Last week, he was having lunch with one of them—his third such lunch this month. He thought things were going well, but right after the manager finished his meal, he grabbed his coat and got up to leave. On his way out, the manager commented that he wasn't sure he was of any help, and Andy doesn't seem like the manager type.

Andy wouldn't have thought anything of it, but later that day his own manager called him into his office and asked him why he seemed distracted lately. Apparently, a few of Andy's co-workers mentioned that Andy didn't have time to help them like he usually does. Furthermore, one co-worker blamed her mistake on Andy because he hadn't taken the time to thoroughly explain her part in their project. Andy's supervisor said that he was surprised to hear people complain about him, when normally he is a valued team member.

Andy begins to question his goal of getting promoted, as now he is not at all sure he has what it takes. As Andy just learned about the concept of **MeYouQ**, he begins to wonder if the problem is not that he doesn't have what it takes, but his behavior instead.

Andy would like to build his **MeYouQ** because he read that it is the key to building strong relationships, and he does want to have better relationships with those at work so he can become a manager one day. Because he seems to be coming across the wrong way to his colleagues, he decides to start looking at the various aspects of himself as an OTHER.

Thinking about the type of person Andy is, go through the questions below and write out some things he could discover about himself as an OTHER. When you are done, read on further to see some suggested answers.

Which of Andy's behaviors might need to be improved in this situation?

- ☐ Professionalism
- ☐ Confidence
- ☐ Stretch his capabilities
- ☐ Approachability
- ☐ Political behavior
- ☐ Leadership
- ☐ Manners/etiquette
- ☐ Helpfulness
- ☐ Fairness and cooperation
- ☐ Respect for others
- ☐ Inclusiveness
- ☐ Patience
- ☐ Communication sending
- ☐ Active listening
- ☐ Use of "I" language
- ☐ Giving feedback
- ☐ Accepting feedback
- ☐ Conflict resolution

How can this mindfulness give him a sense of direction in how he pursues his goal of being a manager? _____

_____

_____

_____

What are the next few steps Andy should take? _____

_____

_____

_____

When Andy is struggling like he is in this case, he can examine the role he could be playing in the situation. He might analyze his own behavior this way:

"What happened at lunch to cause the manager to leave right away? Was I acting unprofessionally in some way? Maybe the manager thought I was being too political and he didn't like my tactics? Do the managers feel like I am using them to get ahead? What type of etiquette is expected at a business lunch? Did I look clumsy? Why would the manager say that I don't have what it takes? Am I coming across as overconfident? Do I need more experience in a certain area? Why am I allowing my pursuit of being manager to interfere with my regular duties? Isn't it going to detract from how people see me as a manager, if I can't communicate project instructions to a co-worker? Do I look like I am not very helpful now? Was I disrespectful in some way to the manager or my co-workers? Could I have done more to communicate effectively, including listening to the team? How can I fix this problem and avoid further conflict? Should I say anything? How can I use "I" language and conflict resolution styles effectively, so I can repair these relationships?"

These types of questions will help Andy to narrow down the potential errors in his behavior and be mindful about his situation. He will be able to choose the most suitable behavior in light of this new awareness. He may see that he does have the skills to be a supervisor, but could choose different courses of action to reach his goal.

You can look at your own situations in a similar manner. When you can recognize the behaviors you use around others that might not be serving you well, you can work to consciously choose more appropriate ones. You will feel more comfortable and be more successful when you are in better control of your actions.

To be able to pinpoint the source of your behavior, you need to know yourself better. Gain a little more practice in building your self-awareness by thinking about some of the aspects of you as an OTHER you just discovered. Begin to recognize your behavior better by answering the following questions:

What impression do you want others to form about you, and what are you going to do to facilitate this? _____

_____

_____

How will your life improve by doing this? _____

_____

List two of your bad manners (perhaps cutting people off when they are speaking) that you are going to work on and how you are going to do this. _____

_____

_____

How will your life improve by doing this? _____

_____

List two things you want to change about your communication
style and what you are going to do to improve. _____

_____

_____

How will your life improve by doing this? _____

_____

Continue to explore your different behaviors until you have a
very good sense of awareness and are regularly mindful about
them. Work to choose the best behaviors for the situation as
much as possible.

In all of this, do not forget to love and understand yourself as
a unique individual. Don't be so critical of yourself or wish to be
someone different, simply be conscious of, and adjust your
behavior as necessary. This will become easier over time as you
are doing more and more things correctly. You will attain more
success and peace in your interactions with others and achieve
more in your life.

You now have many skills in *Knowing and Managing Yourself*.
Take this new self-awareness into Part 2 of *MeYouQ*: *Reserving
Judgment and Showing Empathy*. Just as you can learn to accept
and love yourself, you can learn to accept and appreciate other
people as unique individuals, with a variety of traits that explain
why they think what they think and do what they do.

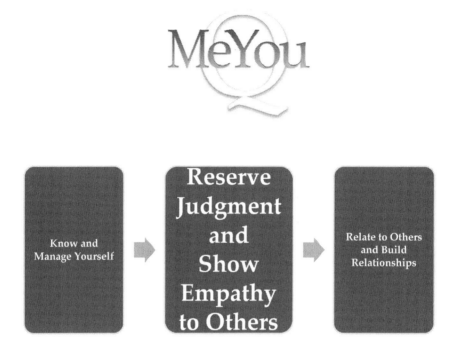

Know and
Manage Yourself

Reserve
Judgment
and
Show
Empathy
to Others

Relate to Others
and Build
Relationships

Part 2: Reserve Judgment and Show Empathy

IN THIS SECTION, YOU WILL CARRY the idea of accepting yourself and understanding why you do the things you do, to also accepting others and understanding why they do the things they do. This requires that you are not quick to jump to conclusions about a person, and that you practice acceptance of differences. This approach will help you avoid some of the frustrations you are having with others, as you become mindful about the ways you judge, learn to appreciate the uniqueness of people, and come to value people, even when they appear very different from you.

> **Reserve Judgment and Show Empathy to Others**
>
> - Keep an open mind and avoid judgment of people because of their actions
> - See others as unique individuals who do what they do because of their various traits
> - Value and respect others just as you value and respect yourself

Chapter 16: Keep an Open Mind and Avoid Judging People because of Their Differences

Do you jump to conclusions about others and judge them unfairly?

THIS STEP IN THE *MeYouQ* PROCESS begins with keeping an open mind and avoiding judgment of people because of their differences. Many times, communication is doomed before it even gets started, and relationships never have a chance to form. When someone says or does something you don't like, or that differs from what you know, you might jump to a conclusion about the type of person they are, how much they know, or what they are capable of doing. You might measure the worth of others according to your own personal characteristics and not appreciate people who are different from you as much as those who are like you. If you could surround yourself with only people who were similar to you, judging people would not be a problem, but most people cannot control their lives to that degree. It is more realistic to develop strategies for building relationships with all kinds of people. You will learn more about this in the last part of the *MeYouQ* process, but for now, work on keeping an open mind about others.

Think about the last time you had negative thoughts about someone after an encounter with him or her. Perhaps you thought the person was weird, or a complainer, or selfish.

154

Whatever it was, if you had a thought like this, you may have judged that person unfairly. People instinctively and automatically judge one another but when that judgment gets in the way of building a relationship with someone, it is dysfunctional. When people go through life without being conscious of their thoughts and actions, they are more likely to misjudge someone. It is important to notice when your mind is reacting to a situation and cast the judgment aside. Instead of rushing to conclusions, you can keep an open mind and search for more information about the individual. Learn what the person is really like, instead of basing your opinion on the one small glimpse you received.

Are you ready to get out of your comfort zone of reaction and become active in your perceptions instead? *MeYouQ* is about choosing your thoughts and behaviors so you can build relationships with a variety of people. Gain control of your mind; catch it judging and decide to be open-minded instead. If you are unable to recognize your mind judging others, start by catching yourself when you gossip or complain about someone else. If you can stop yourself from "negative speak," you will then be able to challenge your mind to think differently about different people in different situations. Practice this now.

Think about the last person you thought or spoke negatively about. What conclusion had you come to about this person? What label did you give him or her? _____

_____

_____

Was that a fair assessment? Do you think there is more to this person than that one aspect? What others stories could you tell yourself about him or her? _____

_____

_____

Perhaps you don't know this person very well. What could you do to learn more about him or her? _____

_____

_____

Humans want validation from others for their thoughts, values, and behaviors; many people need to feel that what they are thinking or doing is the right thing. When people hear or see something that conflicts with their own beliefs, they may try to prove they are right and the others are wrong. This can be what your mind is doing, and you might not be aware of it. Learn to check in with the voice in your head, and notice the games it might be playing.

In the first part of the *MeYouQ* process, you worked on getting to know yourself better and understanding why you behave the way you do. Now, apply the same tools to be conscious of your thoughts regarding other people. Control your thoughts and judgments, and work to appreciate other people as unique individuals with a variety of traits, while you work to understand why they do what they do.

Becoming conscious of and being able to challenge your thoughts may be difficult. Learn to recognize your triggers. These are things you find annoying that cause you to jump to judgment. If you can see that many of these "annoying" behaviors in others are just part of who that person is, you might be more forgiving. Consider the ideas we have covered so far:

- A person might be frustrating to work with because they use a different process to approach a situation. This person may have a different personality type than you (Chapter 1).
- Someone might be dramatic all the time. This person could be low in emotional intelligence (Chapter 2).
- One person may be very boisterous, while another might be constantly worried about what others think. These behaviors may be a reflection of their self-esteem (Chapter 3).
- If someone can't make a decision, or their wacky ideas get them into trouble, it could be their creativity causing them to behave that way (Chapter 4).
- A person who just can't seem to relax, or who bothers you with silly questions might have issues surrounding anxiety (Chapter 5).
- Perhaps one person only cares about money and not about relationships; this could be an issue of different values (Chapter 6).
- A person seems "lost." She often quits what she starts. This behavior might have something to do with her unfulfilled needs (Chapter 7).
- Someone regrets past behavior and can't seem to get over it. Another person holds grudges and is vengeful. These

people may be lacking a sense of spirituality (Chapter 8).

- If someone complains often, is sluggish, or groans frequently; he might be experiencing a feeling of unwellness (Chapter 9).
- One person might be awkward, or miss social cues on how to behave. Another seems to know it all and perhaps insults you. These behaviors might stem from their past experiences (Chapter 10).
- A person who is always critical may be prone to a negative attitude (Chapter 11).
- If one person believes that something should be fixed, and refuses to use it until it is, while another thinks it is "good enough" as is, they probably have different personal standards (Chapter 12).
- Someone who is ingratiating himself with the boss, or going overboard with the role he is playing might be trying to manage impressions (Chapter 14).
- Someone who doesn't get along with others, or seems to do the wrong thing at the wrong time might have an issue with etiquette or manners (Chapter 15).
- Behaviors like being a poor listener, interrupting, blaming others, or being unnecessarily stubborn might be issues involving communication style (Chapter 16).

People do many different things because of their individual traits. While these behaviors may be different from what you would do in the same situation, try not to let these things make you too upset. Remember, it is easy to judge and criticize, but those negative feelings are not going to help you build relations with others. Keep an open mind about a person regardless of their behavior. Attribute the behavior to the trait and not to some intention you think the person might have.

Also recognize when you are jumping to judgment of others in order to protect your own ideas, values, and behaviors. Refrain from judgment and be objective in the situation. Open yourself up to the idea that the other person has his or her own way of looking at the world and could have something to offer you, not that they are trying to be better than you. Be careful of the stories you tell yourself; they might close the door on new ideas and relationships. Consider the following scenarios and see how you could tell a new story, a positive one.

Roberta is assertive with and excited about her ideas, but you think she is a know-it-all.

Tell a new story, a positive one: _Roberta may have some good suggestions, and she was raised to be confident. She isn't trying to be better than everyone else, she just believes in her ideas._

Try these ones on you own:

Charlotte has many ideas but doesn't take part in the detailed operational planning. Her co-workers think she is lazy and just waits for them to do the work.

Tell a new story, a positive one: _____

_____

_____

Sydney is too social at work. She complains she has too much work to do, but she wastes much of her time visiting others.

Tell a new story, a positive one: _____

_____

_____

Theo never helps others at work. He says his co-workers should be responsible for themselves because they are qualified, and they are all getting paid the same. He is not a team player.

Tell a new story, a positive one: _____

_____

_____

Johan lacks focus. Often he forgets to fill out all of his paperwork. He will be working on one task and then jump to something else before the first task is completed. He is too distracted to be productive.

Tell a new story, a positive one: _____

_____

_____

The idea here is not to label people as lazy or distracted, but to see the personal characteristic that is causing the behavior. Additionally, the person may not be working in the area of her strengths, so balance the negative by reminding yourself of the positive qualities and behavior.

What positive stories did you create?

Charlotte is a visionary and should spend her time being innovative because that is her strength. Other, more detail-oriented people will create better operational plans than she could. Those people would be happy to work using their strengths, and Charlotte could spend her time creating new concepts instead.

Sydney is outgoing and values relationships. She spends time with people and would do anything to help them. When she needs help, they will be there for her as well. She has the ability to bring people together, which is important in a team environment. Her time is not being wasted. She might like to have tasks that involve more interaction with others instead.

Theo values equality. He might be feeling taken advantage of for some reason. He sets a high standard for work behavior, which is a positive thing. Theo may actually work well with others when he feels they are doing their fair share. He might appreciate a discussion about workload.

Johan might have a few things going on in his situation. He may be interested in many different aspects of the company. He also might have a hard time saying, "No" when people ask him for help, so he is spread too thin amongst tasks. If Johan knew the priorities for his work, he might be able to focus on a particular task until its completion.

Some of the behaviors in the previous scenarios may have reminded you of situations at work where you got upset with someone. Do you have certain triggers in terms of behaviors in others that really bother you? These types of behaviors; such as people being lazy, thinking they know everything, or being unable to get their work done, may be particularly annoying to you. Work to discover what your triggers are, as these behaviors may cause you to jump to judgment about a person very quickly. When you notice one of these trigger behaviors, remind yourself to keep an open mind about the person. Remind yourself also that getting upset is not good for your own mental health and stress levels. The overall goal of *MeYouQ* is to give you a way to deal with different people effectively, so you do not get too frustrated.

Keeping an open mind is difficult enough on its own, but becomes even more difficult if you are surrounded by negativity. Recognize when the people around you are judging others, and work on keeping your mind open instead. If your co-workers gather around to gossip, simply excuse yourself from the conversation. If you find it difficult to remove yourself, kindly ask them to try to be more positive. Explain to others that the negative chatter and gossip are causing you stress at work, and you need a more positive atmosphere, which will be good for everyone. You can also try to lead by example, and encourage others to have an open mind, recognizing it is not easy to change the behavior of other people. If negativity still surrounds you, make every effort to not internalize the feelings of others.

Separate your sense of being from theirs and do not take on their gloom or pain. Work to ignore the negativity that spews out of the mouths of those around you.

Is it ever ok to judge others? You may have to, at times, in order to facilitate decision making; for example, if you have to pick the best person for the job, or decide if someone is eligible for a reward. Hopefully, you will be able to keep an open mind about a person and be fair, as you judge them according to a set standard. If someone is not measuring up to this standard time and again, you might want to get to know the person better and see what is going on. Work to uncover her strengths, so you can move her into a role where she can be more successful. In some cases, the person might not be a good fit, and you will have to end the relationship, this applies to your personal life as well. In your pursuit of having high *MeYouQ*, remember: Do not put everyone ahead of yourself at your own expense. Your *MeYouQ* journey is about you and your mental health just as much as it is about treating others well. Good mental health will serve you in terms of appreciating others and building relationships with them.

Build your MeYouQ by changing the stories you tell yourself about others and keeping an open mind about them.

> **Chapter 16 Takeaways:**
>
> As you are growing your *MeYouQ* and working towards building healthier relationships, keep an open mind, and avoid judging people because of their actions by:
>
> ↗ Learning to manage your mind just as you manage your behavior
>
> ↗ Catching your mind jumping to judgment and have an open mind instead
>
> ↗ Searching for more information and working to uncover a person's strengths
>
> ↗ Recognizing judgment can prevent relationships from forming; if you have to judge, be objective
>
> ↗ Accepting differences and telling positive stories about others

In the spirit of having an open mind about people and recognizing they have their own strengths and weakness, learn to appreciate a variety of other things about them as well. When you embrace differences, you can find a way to relate to each person, and approach them on an individual level.

Chapter 17: See Others as Unique Individuals Who Do What They Do because of their Various Traits

Do you believe there are many different ways to do the same thing?

HOPEFULLY BY NOW YOU ARE BEING EASIER on yourself and are better able to see why you do the things you do, or at least realize that it's because of some inherent quality. In the same way you developed this awareness about yourself, you can develop an awareness of others.

Recognize the people in your life are all unique individuals, with traits that have come from many different areas of their lives. Understand the influence of these traits on their behaviors, and remember that if people are not consciously choosing their actions, their minds, habits, or impulses will choose for them. While you cannot manage others' behavior for them, you can accept that if they had *MeYouQ*, they would be better able to manage their own behavior. While this doesn't excuse a person for inappropriate behavior, it can help you to get to know the person and treat them as an individual. When you look at each person as unique, you can work on relating to him or her better (which will be covered in the next part of the book).

165

People are all born into particular circumstances and with certain natural tendencies. They didn't get to choose how they were brought up, nor did they have a choice whether or not to go through many of the experiences they had in life. These factors have impacted their traits, which in turn influence their behavior and cause them to do things that other people may not do in the same situation.

Can you allow everyone to express themselves naturally? Can you work to accept all kinds of different behaviors, within reason, as long as people are trying hard and not hurting anyone? Or are you the type of person who believes there is one "right way" to do things? If this describes you, can you stretch your comfort zone to accept other possibilities, so that you may care for your own mental health and be able to relate to others better? Acceptance will reduce stress and conflict for everyone.

If you are of the mindset that your way is the best way, it will serve you to open your mind to the idea that other ways are just as valid as your own. Humans are constantly adapting best practices into their own methods and sometimes do come up with even better ways of doing things. As you open your mind to different methods, you will be receptive to the different traits people have as well. This is speaking in general, however, recognize there are some times when things need to be done a certain way, such as setting a banquet table for example.

A person may not be able to change the way he is, but he can work to change what he does. If a person is not interested in changing, or not aware of how to change, he might be more of a challenge to deal with. You, then, can change how you approach the situation. Many people call this "taking the high road." You can learn how to work with that person's habits better. Consider the following example of working within the confines of someone else's traits:

Alex doesn't like being told what to do. If he didn't come up with the idea, he refuses to go along with it. When you try to explain the merits of your idea to him, he refutes every point. He is becoming ineffective in his job because he just won't listen to feedback. You don't want to fire him, because he is good at his job in other ways. If he could change this behavior, he would be a great employee and team member.

How to work with Alex. Alex is not open to ideas and you need him to be. Is there any way you can take his idea and build on it so it looks more like yours? You may have to accept his idea first, while not revealing yours. Give him positive feedback on the idea and ask him how it can be modified to better work towards a goal you have in mind. While he is modifying the idea, you can encourage the suggestions that go in the direction you have in mind. If most of the plan seems to be from him, he might be open to adding in a few of your suggestions. The issue for you is that this is going to take more time, so you will have to decide if the alternative is better: terminate him, upset the department, lose an employee who is good in other ways, and have to hire and train a new employee. Many times supervisors jump to firing someone as the only solution, when they might be able to work with a person's characteristics instead.

Think about how you should handle the following situations:

Valentin cannot move off of a topic until it's settled. You have noticed that he will make his point over and over again, trying to convince his co-workers to agree with him. Even when the team has agreed to set the issue aside for now and come back to it later, Valentin cannot seem to move on; he has this habit of holding the team back. Everyone else is fine with postponing the discussion, but he keeps bringing it up.

Explain how you would work with Valentin: _____

_____

_____

Clement tends to get emotional. If someone does something he doesn't agree with, he becomes very angry. He seems unable to step outside of the situation and control his emotions. When he gets involved in a situation like this, he remains angry until he can distract himself with shopping or video games. You actually saw him literally snap out of his bad mood after ordering a new game from an online store.

Explain how you would work with Clement: _____

_____

_____

The idea here is to get to know the unique characteristics about others, so you can determine the best way to approach them and get them to behave a certain way for you. This is not about the isolated incidents in these examples; it is about the behavior that is being repeated because it's just who the person is and how he operates.

How did you say you would work with the people in the examples above?

With Valentin, you may have to entertain a short discussion to help him feel heard. Ask him what he would like to see in order for him to move on to the next team task. Perhaps he needs to be reassured that the issue will be handled, so develop a follow-up plan with a deadline to show that you are committed to revisiting the situation. Once you have shown you support Valentin, ask for his cooperation in moving on.

With Clement, you may have to accept that he is going to be in a bad mood for the rest of the day until he can unwind at home. Work to ignore the negative things he says or does for the remainder of the day, and just know that tomorrow will be a new day. Grant him the time he needs to get over the situation in the way he is most comfortable. This may be a great solution, except if Clement has to work with others in a pleasant manner. In these situations, you will have to ask him to hide his emotions for the time being. Acknowledge that you understand he is not happy, but remind him that he has a job to do.

Why should you treat these people this way? Is it wrong to just tell someone to stop doing what they are doing? Alex should stop being selfish about his ideas, Valentin should just get off the topic, and Clement should snap out of his bad mood. How do you think they would react if you said those things to them? If you can accept that people are the way they are, you can create an environment where they feel accepted and not picked on or challenged. This is a holistic approach, where people can be their authentic selves and contribute with their own abilities. Isn't that what you want as well? To be accepted for who you are and not to have people trying to change you all the time?

As an added bonus, when you work with a person's characteristics instead of getting angry with her, you will do a lot for your own mental health. You will have more cooperation and less friction in your environment. If you can be mindful in these situations, you will be able to treat each person with empathy, to accept that they are who they are, just as you are who you are.

Build your MeYouQ by accepting that people do things differently, and work within the constraints of their habits and individual characteristics.

Chapter 17 Takeaways:

As you are growing your *MeYouQ* and working towards building relationships, you see others as unique individuals who do what they do because of their various traits by:

↗ Treating people as individuals and getting to know their unique traits; you will have less friction and more cooperation

↗ Accepting that there are many different ways to do the same thing; opening up to different methods will help you open up to different people

↗ Allowing people to be their authentic selves; learning to work within the confines of their traits instead of demanding they act a certain way all the time

You have a new awareness about treating people in a manner that is going to work for them. Take this concept further now, to not only tolerate differences, but to accept them, and value each human being as having a purpose in this life.

Chapter 18: Value and Respect Others Just as You Value and Respect Yourself

Are you ready to accept others as you accept yourself?

IF YOU DON'T YET VALUE AND RESPECT yourself as being a unique individual with a variety of traits, you might want to go back and work through *Part 1: Know and Manage Yourself*. It will be difficult for you to value and respect others if you don't value and respect yourself first.

Perhaps you value yourself, but you have not really thought about the value of other people. Humans can be competitive by nature, and this might be true for you. If you feel you are better than, or tend to compare yourself to others, it will be difficult for you to value them. As discussed earlier, you will need to remain conscious of your thoughts, and keep an open mind about those you interact with.

How can you care for other people and build relationships if you don't see each individual as valuable? The answer is: you can't. So if you value and respect yourself, it's time to work on valuing and respecting others.

Valuing Others. Ideally, you value yourself as having a purpose on this earth or a gift to share. If you believe this about yourself, you can now value others for having a purpose and something of their own to share. This is "meaning of life" type thinking, but since you will probably never know the meaning of life, maybe you can accept there's a meaning for your life and for the lives of everyone else. It is healthy to think this way, instead of believing that life does not matter. Chapter 8 discussed recognizing that people are in your life for a reason; that you are supposed to learn something from them. Keep that in mind as you look for the value in others.

When you find other people annoying, it is going to be difficult to see them as valuable. Start, then, by thinking of all humans as having value. If you can adopt a general belief that people have potential, that they are sources of knowledge and ideas, that they play an important role in caring for others, or that they are in your life for a particular reason; you will be more accepting of others and better able to see their value, even when they are different from you.

Now you can move from the general mindset that people are valuable, to treating each individual with value. Then go the next step and learn about them and what their unique value proposition is. To help you do this, have a look at your own value proposition first, and list the things that make you valuable; for instance, you might be good at bringing comfort to others, be innovative, have a strong work ethic, or possess a positive attitude. Interestingly enough, these sound like the traits from Part 1. Go ahead and list your strengths now—the things that would be an asset to any group or organization.

What value do you bring to the table? _____

_____

_____

_____

_____

_____

_____

Now that you are aware of the value in yourself, it's time to look at valuing another person. Choose a person you like and a person you don't like, and list the values for each of them.

What value does the person you like bring to the table? _____

_____

_____

_____

_____

_____

_____

What value does the person you don't really like bring to the table? (Come on, try hard to see the value. If you can't see it immediately, spend a bit of time getting to know this person and come back to the question later.) _____

_____

_____

_____

_____

Now that you have practice, list the value of another person you aren't as close to. _____

_____

_____

_____

_____

Great job! Doesn't it feel good to be so positive? To see the good in others? If you can approach every person this way, you will feel better about being around him or her each day. You will be less stressed and better able to build relationships (still coming in the next part of the book). Seeing the value in a person is great; showing her respect is how you will acknowledge her value.

Respecting Others. People show respect for themselves by taking care of their physical, mental, and spiritual well-being. They watch what they eat, behave in a safe and appropriate manner, and exercise regularly. They take time to relax, connect with their inner selves, and spend time with loved ones. The ways you respect yourself are personal to you; each person has his own approach.

If someone was going to show respect to you, how would you want him to do that? Should he feed you good food and take you out for a run? While another person can respect your physical self by not doing anything to harm you physically, it's more likely that he will respect your mental self. He would show respect for your feelings, choices, ideas, opinions, beliefs, and what's important to you.

List the specific ways you would want someone to show you respect: _____

_____

_____

_____

The next time you are out with others, ask them the same question. See if people like to be respected in different ways. Someone might say she doesn't like to be teased, whereas you don't mind being teased. Another person might say he likes you to put your phone down when you are talking to him, something you wouldn't have thought to do. Collect this information about others and see the different boundaries people have. One way most people like to be respected is to not be bumped into, or treated as though they're not even there. If you can become more absorbed in others, people around you will feel respected.

Becoming absorbed in others. Self-absorbed people seem oblivious to what is going on around them. Have you ever watched someone walk through a crowd and cut people off or bump into them, completely unaware of what is going on around them? Have you noticed people who talk on the phone or text when they are in a group? Some individuals just don't act as though other people are around at all.

Have you noticed that few people feel a sense of obligation to others anymore? For example, they say they are going to come to a person's party but then they decide to do something else at the last minute. It seems difficult to count on anyone these days; you have an expectation, and you are disappointed.

Do you know some people who just talk about themselves all the time? They are so excited to show you the new thing they bought, or tell you what they are up to, but they rarely ask you what's new with you. You know everything about their lives, but you wonder how much they actually know about yours.

How do you feel about these behaviors? When people show very little attention to others around them, does it bother you? Maybe not, but it could bother someone else. If you are going to build relationships, you are going to have to become absorbed in others.

When you share the same space at work, you are around each other all the time. You can interact purposefully with other people and contribute to a positive atmosphere. Remember to do more active listening than talking. Remember to think about your shared space and make room for others to join in and use the space also.

Remember to do what you say you're going to do when someone is counting on you. If you are not prepared to uphold a commitment, then don't make it in the first place. Use your skills in assertiveness to say, "I understand the recital is important to you, but I cannot commit to going," or, "Thank you for the invite to your party, but what I really need right now is some quiet time on the couch." Consider, however, that people in your life are right to have expectations sometimes. You will have to commit to them occasionally, even if you don't really feel like it. If someone invites you to a noon hour presentation and you say, "Sounds good," it implies that she can expect you to be there.

Think of the last conversation you had. Did you do more listening or more talking? Did you ask questions about the other person? You might think it's difficult to ask about others because they are so busy asking about you, but if you are conscious and present in the conversation, you can look for opportunities to ask questions about the other person. This will help you to be engaged in the conversation and show you care. Be sure to remember the things he told you about himself as well!

Think of the last time you were out at the mall or the grocery store. Were you aware of others around you? Did you make small talk with anyone? If someone needed help, did you reach out and assist them? An awareness of what is going on around you will allow you to see little opportunities to make a person's day special that do not take much effort at all. These actions are good practice in public, and become even more important around people you are going to want a relationship with.

There are general ways you can show respect to people, but if you can get to know how they show respect to themselves, you can see what's important to them and connect to those specific aspects. For example, some people want you to listen to their problems and give suggestions on how to solve them, whereas others just want you to listen and not give your advice. When you treat people the way _they_ want to be treated, you will be able to move forward in building a relationship with them.

Choose a person you don't know very well and ask him or her what makes them feel respected. List the ways here: _____

_____

_____

_____

You can see how knowing this about a person will allow you to treat her the way she wants to be treated. As you value a person for her special gifts and show respect in a manner she will appreciate, you can move on to building a good relationship with her. This is so important in our world today; especially for people leaders who need to build teams, grow employees, and get results.

Build your MeYouQ by seeing the value in others and treating them in the manner they expect.

Chapter 18 Takeaways:

As you are growing your *MeYouQ* and working towards building relationships, you value and respect others just as you value and respect yourself by:

↗ Seeing the unique value that you and every other individual brings to this world

↗ Recognizing the way you like to be respected can be different from the way others prefer

↗ Discovering what makes people feel respected and treating them the way they want to be treated

↗ Paying attention to others around you and respecting personal boundaries

You can now manage your own thoughts and behaviors and recognize that others will have their own ways of thinking and doing things as well. It's time to move on to Part 3, where you will learn how to connect with others, so that you can build productive relationships.

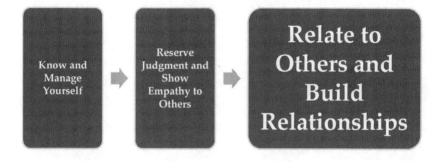

Part 3: Relate to Others and Build Relationships

IN THIS SECTION, YOU WILL MOVE from being open-minded about, and accepting of others, to building relationships with them. You will set the intention to see people in a positive light and get to know them a little more personally. As a people leader, you commit to giving equal attention to people who are like you as well as people who are different. As you get to know your staff better, you strive to develop a working relationship with them. This relationship will be a partnership of give and take, one of support and open communication. Finally, as you are careful not to take people for granted or be taken for granted, you nurture the relationship and fix it when necessary.

Building relationships is not optional in the world today. In whatever capacity you are working with others, it is important to connect with them. This helps you to work together better, and it also gives people that sense of community, and being valued that is so important to fulfilling their individual needs. The relationships you form will help you to meet your needs and achieve your goals as well. This area may be a little more challenging because you need the other person to reciprocate in relationship-building activities. If things do not work at first, keep trying!

Get ready for your life to change as you move forward with a genuine desire to have better relationships and commit to building productive partnerships.

Relate to Others and Build Relationships

- Make the decision to build the relationship and determine how to relate
- Discover your role in, and work hard towards building a productive working relationship

Chapter 19: Decide to Build the Relationship and Determine How to Relate

How much effort are you putting into building relationships?

YOU HAVE ALREADY REFLECTED ON knowing yourself and seeing all humans as unique individuals who do what they do because of their various traits. You practiced being non-judgmental and valuing people as having some role to play in this life, and possibly in your life. As you practice *MeYouQ*, you are hopefully seeing that people should be able to behave appropriately for the situation without having to change who they are.

With this understanding in mind, you can begin to build relationships with all kinds of people. Because everyone in your life is different, you will need to approach each individual in a unique way, getting to know more about the person and what you need to do to get along with him or her. Instead of waiting for this to happen on its own, you can take the initiative to approach people and get things started.

Choose the person. Many relationships begin because people occupy physical space in close proximity. You meet your co-workers and your neighbors; you like some of them and choose to associate with them, while you associate less with those you don't seem to have anything in common with. These relationships are easy, but not necessarily ones you would choose to have if they weren't so convenient.

List the people at work with whom you have a good relationship (not just rapport, but an actual relationship): _____

_____

_____

_____

Who at your work is not on this list? _____

_____

_____

_____

If you want to build a relationship with someone, and it hasn't happened naturally, you need to decide to go out of your way to do it. As a human being, you can look at WIIFM (discussed earlier), and pursue relationships with people that have something to offer you. When you begin to think of what makes life great—new points of view, interesting stories, humor, support, etc.—you can see that many people have something to offer you. As a people leader, you should be looking to build relations with ALL members of your team, other managers, and various stakeholders. As a people leader, you should be looking at *What's In It For My* Team Member. Each of your team members is going to need something from you at some point in time. You will understand their needs when you get to know them better, and they can only have their needs met when they feel comfortable asking for your help.

When you move to Part 4 of the book, you will see a variety of ways to provide for employees' psychological health and safety. In order to provide these things, you first have to build good working relationships. It is your duty to initiate a relationship with each person who works for you, whether you initially like that person or not. So first, set the intention to have the relationship; then adopt a positive mindset as you do the tough work.

Frame your thinking. As you prepare to get to know someone better and uncover her strengths, remind yourself of *MeYouQ Part 2: Reserve Judgment and Show Empathy.* Prepare to approach the individual with the goal of finding a commonality. Having something in common with them will give you a starting point for building a positive relationship, if in fact you do have something in common. The idea is to build a bridge to the other person—a common interest or aspect of your life. This will be a positive factor to begin building the relationship upon.

Finding what you have in common with someone should be fairly easy. You can engage in some small talk as a hallway conversation, or invite the person for a coffee. Be careful not to infringe upon their privacy, especially with human rights-categorized information where people don't want to risk discrimination. Talking about someone's spouse or kids, for example, is not appropriate for you to bring up, but if they offer the information first that is fine. Be sure to maintain professional boundaries.

List some things you would share about yourself when engaging in small talk with someone you didn't know very well:

_____

_____

_____

_____

Now keeping in mind that not everyone is like you, which of these topics might be appropriate to bring up with someone you do not know very well? _____

_____

_____

So, now you have some topics to initiate a conversation. You may have come up with hobbies, sports, music, travel experiences, shopping, or other interests. If you cannot find something you are both interested in, you can show interest in something that is important to her. Remember that you want to treat people as they want to be treated; find something the two of you can relate to, or something you can get excited about in the other person. Pay attention to the conversation because you are going to have to remember some details for the future. Keeping a written record of employee interactions is a great idea; you can review the information before you connect with her again.

Name someone you would like to make a connection with: _____

_____

List some things you might talk about with that person: _____

_____

_____

_____

Arrange to spend a little time chatting with the person. Confess that you do not know much about her, and you would like to get to know her better. Ask how her weekend was, or how she's enjoying her job, to get the discussion going. Mentally refer to your list of topics if you are having trouble coming up with things to talk about. Be careful not to overshadow the person's stories with your own. You don't need to match everything she says with something about yourself; be other-oriented. Use your _MeYouQ_ to be positive and non-judgmental. After the conversation, let her know you enjoyed chatting with her, and make some notes on things you talked about, some details she provided, for future reference.

How did the conversation go? What would you do differently next time? _____

_____

_____

_____

This is a great start, and you will need to keep the momentum going until you have built a connection between the two of you. Consider this example:

You have been the supervisor of your department for two months now. It has been a busy time, and you admit you don't really know everyone on your team that well. One of your employees, Liam, does his job well, so you have not had much need to talk to him. You decide it's time to get to know Liam better.

It's the middle of the morning, and the big rush for the day is done. Liam seems to have some free time, so you take the opportunity to strike up a conversation. You ask Liam if he has a minute, and he does. The other employees are in a different area, so you decide to have the conversation right there.

You thank Liam for keeping production running smoothly while you have taken over as supervisor; you can tell he knows his job well. Liam smiles and says that you're welcome. You say that it looks like you will be spending lots of time together at work, you would like to get to know him better, and you ask him what his interests outside of work are. Liam says he likes to play poker, and he is into those big poker competitions. You have no interest in poker, but you have heard of it. Because poker is important to Liam, you decide to learn more about it. You ask Liam if he has won any big pots, or if he plays online, even who is favorite professional player is. You now have more information about Liam which you can use to build on in the future.

This is not just idle conversation; you are beginning to build a bridge between yourself and the other person. Even if talking about things you are not interested in is painful for you, it is

189

important to them, and therefore important for building the foundation of a relationship.

Recognize that many people won't open up until they have a level of trust in you. You can build trust by showing integrity, not gossiping, not speaking ill of others, and doing what you say you will do. People also need to know your intentions are genuine and not feel that you are just trying to get information to use against them in the future. For these reasons, it's best to keep your questioning on a professional level and not delve into someone's personal life, or probe for too much information, until your rapport with them is much better.

Make the connection. Think about a conversation you had with someone you wanted to make a connection with and what they said. What topics could you get interested in, or what did you have in common with that person? Don't forget to keep notes about each of your relationships, so you can keep their details straight. For instance, it would be inexcusable to ask about someone's son when he has a daughter. Memorize a few things about each person, so you can connect with each individual in a meaningful manner in the future. Keep track of whether you have reached out to each one regularly, giving all employees equal attention as much as possible.

Are there people you know who seem to be able to easily connect with others? What do they do that facilitates this? _____

_____

_____

Which of these things comes naturally to you? _____

_____

Which of them requires you to break out of your comfort zone?

_____

Try out a conversation with someone, and reflect on whether you connected. How can you improve? _____

_____

_____

Plan to check in with people with whom you have been out of touch. Talk about things that are important to them, and make it more meaningful than just talking about the weather. Put these interactions on your to-do list, and make it a priority to connect with the people you lead in your work life. Note that it will be difficult to show an interest in them if you feel you don't really care about other people, so if this is how you feel, you will need to work to change your attitude. Caring about other people and making them feel good can add a lot to both of your lives, and if you are a people leader, it is an important part of your job.

> **Name someone you have not talked to for a while and should reconnect with:** _____
>
> **List things you can talk about with this person:** _____
>
> _____
>
> _____

Contact this individual and set a date for the near future. After you meet with the person, update your records to reflect any new information about him or her that came to light. This should be done regularly with the members of your team or department to ensure you have good rapport. Once you have built some camaraderie, you can continue to connect with people by giving them useful feedback.

Give positive feedback. Employees need feedback about their performance (recall the use of positive, corrective feedback from Chapter 15), so you can use these opportunities as another way to bridge the gap in your interests. Instead of being critical, focus the feedback on what he does well. If something is being done incorrectly, simply show him how to do it properly, but do not take the discussion in a negative direction. As a boss, you can convey that you have every confidence in his abilities, and give him attention and development opportunities as appropriate. Most people will respond to this type of feedback by rising to the occasion and becoming a valued employee. If you are not the boss, but you are trying to make a connection with someone, work on vocalizing the great things you notice about them. Tell her the positive traits you see in her.

Try to make your comments meaningful and not superficial. Notice things that matter, those that will make people feel good about who they are, not just what they are wearing or how their hair looks—though sometimes those things are nice to acknowledge as well. Most people do not care that you like their new shoes, they would prefer to be told they are intelligent, caring, or had a great idea. If you can get to know the person better, you will find out what kinds of comments and feedback are meaningful to them. This is how you make connections and show your *MeYouQ*.

Think about compliments you have received. Which ones were the most meaningful to you? _____

_____

_____

_____

Think about someone in your life you would like to compliment. What should you focus on and what will you say? _____

_____

_____

_____

Remember to keep your feedback completely positive. Don't say, *"You are so kind to always jump in and help out, but you could also initiate some activities."* Keep focused on only the positive message, or it will get buried under the negative one. Being gracious, and thanking people for the things they do is also important. Your kind words will go a long way in building relationships, as long as you really mean them.

As time goes on, you can move from small talk and general feedback to building a real relationship. Because you have shown an interest in the person and have been nice to him, he will be more likely to work with you in building a relationship. Your relationship will involve doing things for each other—people who like each other are more likely to support each other this way. If you do not begin your relationship by first relating to and connecting with others, you may have to rely on your authority to convince people to do things. Telling employees they have to listen to you because you are the boss will bring compliance, but not necessarily enthusiasm, or effort. You are better off to build relationships and have people WANT to work hard for YOU.

Many people leaders struggle with wanting to be liked versus wanting to be respected. There are two ways of looking at this issue. On the one hand, managers feel that if they are friends with their subordinates, people will take advantage of them, or they will be accused of playing favorites. On the other hand, will people respect you if they don't like you? If people simply respect your authority, but not you as a person, they are not going to put in that extra effort for you. In some cases, they will rebel and make your life difficult. So, from a *MeYouQ* perspective, it is recommended that you adopt the mindset that you want to be liked by everyone. This might not be possible if the people around you are not open to it, but it is worth the effort. You will have deeper relationships, be happier, and be better able to develop and engage most of your employees.

Build your MeYouQ by reaching out to new people and talking about things that are important to them.

Chapter 19 Takeaways:

As you are growing your *MeYouQ* and working towards building relationships, you make the decision to build the relationship and determine how to relate by:

↗ Reaching out to people on purpose instead of waiting for the connection to build on its own

↗ Approaching people that will benefit from a relationship with you, not just those who you will benefit from

↗ Choosing to make positive connections through meaningful, purposeful small talk

↗ Keeping track of each person's interests and connecting with everyone regularly

↗ Remembering that people will be more productive when they want to, not have to, support you

Chapter 20: Discover Your Role in, and Work Hard Towards Building Productive Working Relationships

What does being a partner in a relationship mean?

AT THIS POINT IN THE *MeYouQ* PROCESS you should be well-positioned to be a good partner in a work or personal relationship. Use the things you have practiced to build productive working relationships with others: know and manage yourself, reserve judgment, show empathy to others, and relate to others as you make meaningful connections.

A good working relationship means communicating openly and assertively, seeing things from the other person's point of view, being accountable, solving problems and making decisions together, giving and receiving equally, being trusting and trustworthy, and showing an interest in the other person. Let's look at each of these areas a little more closely.

Communicating openly and assertively. Open communication means talking about issues that need to be resolved, and not withholding information that should be shared. When you communicate openly, you address issues directly with a person and do not talk about them behind their back to other people. When the conversation is about something you need to have happen, you will want to communicate assertively. Remember assertiveness involves using "I" language to speak up for your needs and wants; for example, "I would like…" or, "I hope I am being clear, I need you to…" This is better than using "you" language, which can sound like you are blaming the other person; for example, "You never help out," or, "You didn't do what I asked." This type of language will result in an argument instead of a productive discussion. You will have the opportunity to practice "I" language in Part 4.

Recall that part of being assertive is realizing that there is a time and a place for assertiveness, and to resolve conflict you do not always have to stand up for what you need. If you decide that you must stand up for your needs, not only should you use "I" language and be respectful, you should ensure you are having the conversation at the right time and place. For example, maybe the conversation should happen in private and after you have had some time to choose your action, instead of reacting to a heated situation. Consider whether it is a good time for the other person as well; he might be trying to meet a deadline and you are interrupting him. From a *MeYouQ* perspective, you can show the other person respect with your communication style. You can also connect more, and encourage him to talk to you about any issues with his job, so that you can help him meet his needs, and match his duties to his strengths where possible.

Seeing things from the other person's point of view. Using the *MeYouQ* process, you should have already come to appreciate that people are unique and have their own points of view, but to build relationships effectively, you also have to work on really understanding their point of view. By using your active listening skills—really listening to people and probing for more information until you understand—you can ensure the other person feels they have been heard. When asking questions, be careful that you are not using a tone or facial expression that would make her feel she needs to defend her view or back down from it. Just work to understand what she is saying and how she feels about it. During these types of conversations, it may not be appropriate to give your view. Sometimes a person just needs to have her say about a situation. Be a good listener, without thinking about what you are going to say next, or judging the point of view. Just listen. If you are able to recall information said in that conversation later, you were listening well.

Be sure to demonstrate empathy. People are often very critical of each other. For some reason they feel their way of doing something is better than everyone else's. Humans are so competitive! Instead of judging others in terms of your own strengths, recognize that all people have their own strengths, and weaknesses. Work to see the strengths in others and draw upon them. Where someone has a weakness, see if you can help balance it with one of your strengths. Be mindful of your standards and the expectations you have of others. Measure them objectively, not in comparison to you. This is going to be easy for you as you develop your *MeYouQ*!

People are also going to go through rough times in their lives, and they will need you to be understanding. Everyone has different demands on his or her life, and no one can possibly know exactly what another person is facing. People also have different levels of resilience, a different ability to cope. Work to see that people may be different from you in this way. Be supportive and accommodating as much as possible.

Instead of becoming angry with someone when they disappoint you, use forgiveness. Work to understand why they did what they did, and allow them to learn from their mistake.

Use your skills in assertiveness to explain how the issue impacted you, without blaming them. As you are compassionate with others, they should treat you the same way when you make a mistake. No one is perfect.

Is there someone who you've been less than empathetic with? What are your beliefs about the situation that make it difficult for you to see it from the other person's point of view? _____

_____

_____

What new story can you tell yourself so you can see the situation from his or her point of view? _____

_____

How can you handle this situation with empathy? What can you say to the person, or do to assist? _____

_____

It's time to put your empathy plan into action. See if you can create an opportunity to approach this situation and build a relationship with this person.

How did your plan work? Were you able to show empathy? What would you do differently next time? _____

_____

_____

Being accountable. Having a good relationship with someone means that you can count on each other. When someone asks you to do something for them, and you say you will, you need to follow through. Sometimes you will be counted upon because of the relationship you have with a person, not because of something you explicitly agreed to do. Doing your fair share, being there for emotional support, or treating the other person fairly, are examples of implicit expectations people may have of you. If you do not live up to this accountability standard, the relationship can quickly deteriorate.

Solving problems and making decisions together. A relationship is a partnership that involves your commitment to work with the other person in easy and difficult times. Emotions can run high in the latter situations, and you need to keep yours in check while you get all the information out in the open. Make it safe for the other person to say what he is thinking. Be able to listen objectively, without getting defensive, even if it seems as though he is blaming you. Remember that you are trying to be respectful, but the other person may not have the same *MeYouQ* skills as you do. Be able to see through any negative emotions or disrespectful things being said, and find the message you need to hear. Once you get to the heart of the problem, you can keep good communication going, while you work together to better understand the situation, and brainstorm possible solutions. Watch for emotional attachment to solutions as well, and make your final decision based on what is best according to your shared criteria. Commit to the decision-making process until a mutually agreed upon solution is found. This may not happen right away, so be patient.

Giving and receiving equally. Every relationship should be a partnership where there is equal give and take. Sometimes you need to support the other person, and sometimes you will be supported. If you are constantly giving or sacrificing for the other person, you may come to resent him; if he is the one always giving, he may resent you. While it is unnecessary to keep a formal score on your exchanges, you should make a mental note of whether you are giving and receiving enough. If you notice you are not giving enough, ask the person what you can do to help. If you are not receiving enough, you will have to figure out exactly what is lacking, and then talk to him about what he is willing to do to help you have your needs met. Recognize that sometimes "giving" means just spending time with a person.

Expressing appreciation. One of the best things you can do for someone else is to show them appreciation. As previously discussed, people have an intrinsic need to feel valued, and expressing gratitude to them can go a long way towards building relations.

No one wants to be taken for granted. When someone works hard, comes up with a new idea, or goes out of their way for someone else, for example, they should be recognized. Recognition does not have to be public, and in fact many people prefer it not be. A simple conversation between the two of you is all that is required. Be aware, however, that just saying, "Thank you" again and again may become meaningless if the person feels you are thanking them just to have them continue to do extra things. Ensure the person feels treated fairly, and that she is happy to do these things, not compelled to do them. When someone thanks you for something remember to share credit with others who were involved.

Showing appreciation for people brings positivity to the environment. When you make someone feel good, it's contagious! They will want to pay it forward and make someone else feel good too. Positivity will spread through your workplace, from person to person, and people will be happy to do extra things.

Who can you show appreciation to and for what? _____

_____

_____

What are you going to say to this person? _____

_____

_____

Now go try it out!

How did it go? Did you make their day? Would you do anything differently? _____

_____

_____

Are you already thinking about the next person you are going to appreciate? Who is it? What are you going to appreciate them for?

_____

_____

_____

Being trusting and trustworthy. A high level of trust is required for a relationship to endure over time. Trusting other people will allow them to be themselves and to develop in their own way. As long as a person has done nothing to break trust, you should have faith that she is doing what she thinks is best. Avoid suspicion, or doubting that she will do the right thing. Instead, showing trust will strengthen your relationship and encourage the other person to trust you. Being trustworthy means you do what you say you will do, and what is expected of you. It is realistic to have expectations of others. In a relationship you should be able to count on the other person supporting you, speaking positively about you, taking your concerns seriously, and being truthful.

Showing an interest in the other person. You can strengthen your relationships by continuing to show an interest in each other. People love to talk about themselves and to have someone listen. This means continuing to take the time to connect with others and not taking the relationship for granted. Make them feel important. The extent to which someone needs to talk about themselves, and how much they wish to share differs greatly, so gauge your interactions accordingly. If you determined in Part 1 that you are introverted, spending more time with others is going to take an extra effort from you.

If you are not being paid enough attention in this regard, you may begin to feel that you are not important. If you would like a little attention for your interests, slowly try to draw the other person into a conversation, without overwhelming her, or taking up too much of her time. Do not act "needy," just let the person know you would like to share something with her. The amount of information people are comfortable knowing about you will vary, so pay close attention to these interactions as well, you don't want to overstep the boundaries. Recall self-monitoring abilities from Part 1; you need to gauge how others perceive you.

Think about one of your relationships that does not seem to be going very well. Why is it important to you to repair this relationship? (If it isn't important, choose a different example.)

_____

Look back at the elements of a good working relationship discussed in this chapter. Which factor or factors seem to be the problem? _____

_____

_____

What should you do to fix these problem areas? (Think about what you can do and what you will ask the other person to do.)

_____

_____

_____

Write down what you will say: _____

_____

_____

_____

_____

If you approach the situation with the right intent, explain to the person why the relationship is important to you, and use respectful language, you should then be able to have the type of conversation you need to have in order to fix the problem. Be sure to get the person to think about *"What's In It For Me,"* such as a special mentoring opportunity, so he or she will be committed to working on the relationship with you.

Relationships have to work for both parties. Approaching your relationships with these different goals in mind will help you to balance your needs with the needs of others, while you negotiate and build a respectful approach to getting along and working together. Use your *MeYouQ* skills to remind yourself to choose appropriate behaviors, be non-judgmental, and value the uniqueness of others. Be empathetic, and see things from others' points of view, so you realize what is important to them and how they want to be treated. Know yourself and be assertive, so your own needs are not lost in trying to please others. Remember that others may not have the level of *MeYouQ* that you do; be patient with them, as they may not realize how their personal characteristics are affecting their behavior. Learn how to work with each person's unique traits.

Despite your best efforts, some relationships won't form naturally. If this is the case, let the person know you would like to build a successful work relationship and explicitly discuss with him the whole list of "good working relationship" topics covered in this chapter. This will open the conversation and allow you to determine how you, as partners in the relationship, will handle each area together. These factors are too important to leave to chance in essential relationships.

Build your MeYouQ by holding up your side of the partnership in important relationships.

Chapter 20 Takeaways:

As you are growing your *MeYouQ*, you discover your role in, and work hard towards building productive working relationships by:

↗ Using positive communication skills to have discussions that need to occur

↗ Seeing things from the other person's point of view

↗ Being the type of person others can trust and count on

↗ Making decisions and solving problems together

↗ Balancing give and take in the relationship

↗ Giving attention to, and showing an interest in others

↗ Openly discussing problems in the relationship

↗ Remembering that not everyone has skills in *MeYouQ*

How is your development coming along? Take the *MeYouQ* Self-Assessment again before moving on to Part 4.

Behavior	+ or -
1. I think about and consciously choose my behavior	
2. I often put the needs of others ahead of my own	
3. I am at peace with who I am; I accept myself	
4. I follow up and do what I say I will do	
5. I ensure my relationships are not one-sided	
6. I generally find people enjoyable and interesting	
7. I would say that, in general, people like me	
8. I often feel very positive and optimistic	
9. People often say nice things about me	
10. I am easily able to see others' points of view	
11. I am open to new ideas and methods	
12. I play and work well with others	
13. I find it easy to show an interest in others	
14. I monitor my behavior and act appropriately	
15. I don't hold grudges when someone has harmed me	
16. I am respectful when addressing difficult issues	
17. I love the people in my life unconditionally	
18. It is ok if people have standards different than mine	
19. I believe each person has a unique gift to share	
20. People understand me the first time I say something	
21. I treat others the way they want to be treated	
22. I value people who are different/think differently	
23. I find it easy to get to know people on a personal level	
24. I believe I am here on earth for a reason	
25. I have many good relationships, personal and work	
Total + Signs	

Total your plus signs. Did you improve since taking the self-assessment for the first time? Where are your weaknesses? Revisit those areas to gain more practice and improve your skills. Growing your *MeYouQ* can take some time, but change is possible when you become aware of the elements of *MeYouQ* and are committed to self-improvement.

Continue to practice your skills with the different people in your life, and visit meyouqbook.com for more ideas (password: pY23tD4c26). Then move on to Part 4, where you will further your development and learn additional life-changing protocols you can use in your career, or personal life, as a people leader. Discover things you can do to care for the well-being of others and develop loyal, engaged employees who want to work hard for you.

Part 4: Use *MeYouQ* to Supervise for Psychological Health and Safety

Do you know what a psychologically healthy environment looks like?

THE JOURNEY TO PSYCHOLOGICAL HEALTH and safety in the workplace begins with *MeYouQ*. You can manage your various traits and behaviors, and you can see that others have their own unique set of traits and behaviors too. Just as you have your idiosyncrasies, others have theirs as well. Hopefully this awareness will encourage you to pay more attention to the effect you have on your employees and the workplace in general, as you refrain from judging others, appreciating their strengths and accommodating their weaknesses.

Employees spend roughly one-third of their lives at work. The work atmosphere they face each day will either positively or negatively impact them mentally and physically. Building a supportive work environment means caring for the mind, body, and spirit of all employees. This environment can be built with good policies and practices in organizations. While supervisors and team leaders may have limited ability to influence policies, they do have a direct impact on employee relations practices.

Many organizations promote employees to leadership positions without giving them a proper orientation to their new responsibilities. The more supervisors can see the importance of playing their leadership role effectively and investing in their own professional development, the happier and healthier employees and workplaces will be. You are halfway there with your awareness of *MeYouQ*. The missing piece is how to implement the basic principles of management.

A psychologically healthy workplace is the employers' and leaders' responsibility! This section of the book will help you become the kind of leader that has a positive impact on employees; someone who can bring out the best in others.

Support for mental health in the workplace focuses on a variety of factors that supervisors can directly affect. These Psychological Factors*, as outlined by Gilbert, Bilsker, Shain & Samra, (2012), in Guarding Minds @ Work[2] are:

1. Psychological Support – A work environment where co-workers and supervisors are supportive of employees' psychological and mental health concerns and respond appropriately as needed.
2. Organizational Culture – A work environment characterized by trust, honesty, and fairness.
3. Clear Leadership & Expectations – A work environment where there is effective leadership and support that helps employees know what they need to do, how their work contributes to the organization, and whether there are impending changes.
4. Civility & Respect – A work environment where employees are respectful and considerate in their interactions with one another, as well as with customers, clients, and the public.

---

[2] https://www.guardingmindsatwork.ca/

5. Psychological Competencies & Requirements – A work environment where there is a good fit between employees' interpersonal and emotional competencies and the requirements of the positions they hold.
6. Growth & Development – A work environment where employees receive encouragement and support in the development of their interpersonal, emotional, and job skills.
7. Recognition & Reward – A work environment where there is appropriate acknowledgement and appreciation of employees' efforts in a fair and timely manner.
8. Involvement & Influence – A work environment where employees are included in discussions about how their work is accomplished and how important decisions are made.
9. Workload Management – A work environment where tasks and responsibilities can be accomplished successfully within the time frame available.
10. Engagement – A work environment where employees feel connected to their work and are motivated to do their job well.
11. Balance – A work environment where there is recognition of the need for balance between the demands of work, family, and personal life.
12. Psychological Protection – A work environment where employees' psychological safety is ensured.
13. Protection of Physical Safety – A work environment where management takes appropriate action to protect the physical safety of employees.

Reprinted with permission

In this part of the book, you will be given strategies for developing your supervisory skills and working effectively with employees, while paying special attention to psychological health and safety factors. You will have the opportunity to develop practical skills in supervision and leadership, but before that, here is some background information on mental health and the workplace.

Chapter 21: Mental Health

How much do you know about the mental health of your employees?

YOUR EMPLOYEES MAY HAVE mental health issues that are impacting their work, or work may be negatively contributing to employee mental health. In the first situation, the workplace needs to be supportive of special needs the employee might have. Organizations do this through Disability Management and Stay-at-Work programs. To help employees with a mental illness stay at work, the idea is to create a pleasant working environment, and practice good employee relations in order to reduce stress and its effects. This final part of the book will have many strategies for you to use to positively impact the mental health of your employees, while carrying out your supervisory responsibilities.

A Disability Management (DM) program is typically used for helping people return to work after an injury or illness. The idea is that the longer an employee is away from work, the lower the chance of her resuming a normal work life. Employees with mental illness may need to be away from work episodically, or for extended periods. The DM program can ensure employees have the time they need and are pointed in the direction of vital support systems. This does not mean that they get paid the whole time they are away, but that they have a job to return to when they are ready to come back. To facilitate an earlier return to

213

work, keep in touch with employees and show you care for their well-being. Offer them reduced-, light-or flexible-work arrangements until they can be at work on a regular basis. A stay-at-work program would use this type of flexible work schedule as a proactive measure, so the employee doesn't have to go on disability leave. With an increasing number of people being diagnosed with mental illness and requiring treatment, more and more organizations will need a plan on how to support them.

There is still a significant social stigma associated with mental health issues therefore people affected by mental illness may be reluctant to discuss their disorder. Employees could be on medication or undergoing other forms of therapy, and they may not want people in the workplace to know for fear that it will make them look weak or incapable. To reduce stigma, supervisors need to be more knowledgeable about mental illness, and be capable of talking to employees about any special accommodations they may require. Supervisors need to understand what mental illness is, and develop empathy for employees who may be dealing with such an issue. As an example, if someone suffers from depression, he may experience days when he can't even get out of bed. A depressed person may not be able to see the positive in anything, or experience any happiness. A person who has never had chronic, severe depression may not be able to empathize; she may try to convince the person with depression that he isn't really depressed, that he just needs to think more positively and try to cheer up. This is not likely to be helpful. While the supervisor may not understand the illness, at least she can be supportive of the employee. While she may not be able to relate to how the person feels, she can do her part to ensure that he can talk about his illness and ask for the help he needs without feeling shame.

Empathy and good listening skills extend to employees who come to you feeling stressed out as well, even if they haven't been diagnosed with a mental illness. Employees need to feel they are able to approach their supervisor with these types of problems and not fear that it is going to make them look weak. Additionally, the supervisor and co-workers should take notice when people appear to have something bothering them. Check in with people; ask them if something is wrong. Encourage them to see their doctor or seek other assistance. Let them know you care.

Becoming mental-health-friendly shouldn't be difficult for you, with your *MeYouQ* skills in knowing yourself and relating to others. Your ability to know, understand, and manage your own characteristics, while working to recognize and understand those of others will continue to help you undertake your role as supervisor, and ensure you can support your employees' psychological health and safety. Primarily, you will want to refrain from judgment, and keep an open mind in these situations.

Move on now to the lessons in management, supervision, and human resources management theory. These lessons are the essence of what is generally taught in similar courses and textbooks. This will be a good background for you to quickly assume your new role. Specific topics to be covered are stress management, leadership, personal management skills, directing the work of others, training, safety, performance management, employee motivation, change management, and dealing with difficult situations.

The basics will be presented, followed by specific actions you can take to ensure you are implementing the theories in a positive, *MeYouQ*, mentally healthy way—the focus being on doing what's best for your employees while meeting the needs of the organization. A positive work environment is one where employees feel good about being at work. It's one where they feel appreciated and valued. In this type of work environment people are treated well and have the opportunity to thrive. Under psychological health and safety, the employer and managers recognize this duty of care to employees.

Chapter 21 Takeaways:

↗ Disability Management programs are used to provide a more caring and supportive atmosphere, and facilitate an earlier return to work

↗ Stay-at-work programs can proactively provide a flexible work schedule for individuals so they don't need to go on extended disability leave

↗ Disability management and stay-at-work programs can be used to support employees dealing with mental health issues

↗ Supervisors need skills to reduce the stigma surrounding mental health in the workplace and to be able to talk with employees about accommodations when mental health issues are affecting their work

---

This positive work environment is one where undue stress does not exist. To understand stress better, you need to understand where it comes from, so strategies for managing stress can be developed.

Chapter 22: Stress Management

Have you noticed that people handle stress differently?

THE FIRST OF THE VARIOUS THEORIES on managing people is stress management because the ability to create a psychologically healthy environment has a lot to do with understanding what causes tension, and how people react to it. A comprehensive discussion on stress includes: stressors, stress, stress moderators, and strain.

Stressors are the things that cause stress, and they are different for each person. While a poor boss may cause stress for everyone in the office, traffic congestion will only be stressful for some people. A crying baby might be cute to family and friends, but a disturbance to everyone else. A looming deadline on a project may be no big deal for some of your employees, but paralyzing for others.

The mental or emotional anxiety resulting from the stressful event is called stress, and it may manifest as a sense of pressure and/or discomfort. These feelings can motivate someone to take action on a project or handle a situation, but stress can also be debilitating—people feel stressed, but they can't, or won't do anything about it. Their reaction is in partnership with the strategies they use for dealing with the stress; these are called stress moderators.

217

Methods of dealing with stress can include: making a to-do list, talking to people, rearranging a schedule, being distracted, eating more, smoking more, drinking more alcohol, developing high blood pressure or headaches, or yelling at people. Some of these are healthy ways of dealing with stress and some are not. Developing positive stress moderators is important to an individual's ability to deal with stress.

Finally, if a person is unable to deal with stress effectively, he may become overstressed, or experience strain. Strain could be the cause in cases where someone is suffering from burnout and feels he can't continue to work, has a health episode like a chest tightening, or can't get out of bed, for instance. At this point, professional help is probably needed to help them recover.

Have a look at the following example that involves a difference in stress reactions and use of stress moderators in employees working alongside each other.

Ethan, Jay, and Matthew work on an assembly line to load press board onto the transfer cart as it comes out of the press. As the board comes out, the lift system picks it up, turns it from a horizontal position to a vertical one and slides it onto the cart. The machine works safely and accurately most of the time, but occasionally it has a small delay which requires workers to pull on the board slightly. It doesn't bother Ethan when this happens; he knows the fix and implements it accordingly. The situation does bother Jay and Matthew, however. It didn't at first, but now it contributes to their stress in the workplace.

Jay finds the machine, in addition to several other things, a stressful part of his job. He doesn't understand why management can't just fix the problems in the factory. He goes to work and does his job, while grumbling about the company. After work, he stops by the beer store for a six-pack so he can relax when he gets home.

Matthew finds a few things stressful at work as well. He doesn't want work to affect his health and happiness, so he deals with his stress by having regular meetings with his manager to let her know about problems that need fixing in the workplace. He believes his boss will get things fixed when she can, and that he needs to be patient in the meantime.

Did you notice that the broken machinery didn't bother all three employees? This is an example that shows stressors are different for different people. Did you also notice that the two people it did bother had different stress moderators for managing their stress? One reacts with a drinking habit, and one tries to effect change while remaining calm and patient. You will be able to see similar differences in your employees; each person experiences stress differently and has different stress moderators.

The lesson to be learned from a *know yourself and relate to others* point of view is that people experience stress under different circumstances, and they have different methods of coping. Recognize that even though you aren't overly stressed, or you can manage your stress in a positive way, this may not be the case for your employees; one group member may be able to handle the work, while another cannot. You may have developed resilience over the years and have a variety of stress moderators that work for you. Others may not have been taught these strategies, or their personal characteristics don't allow them to handle stress as easily.

You can work with your employees to help reduce the number of stressful situations they face. Get to know them and understand what kinds of situations are more suitable for them at work. This isn't to say the people who can't handle stress get all the easy assignments, but perhaps situations known to cause them stress can be minimized. When stress can't be avoided, you can teach them techniques to manage it, remembering that what works for you may not be what works for them. In this way you can show you care for your employees.

Write down an example when you were able to handle stress and one of your co-workers was not. Which stress moderators did you use? _____

_____

What did the other person do? _____

_____

Knowing this person as you do, what might have worked better for him or her as a stress moderator? _____

_____

Applications for Employee Mental Health

The ability to manage stress is important for all 13 Psychological Factors (refer to pages 210 and 211), because they all have the potential to affect employee mental health if not handled correctly. See the examples that follow for Factors 1, 2, 5, and 9.

Psychological Support (PF1) is about supporting employees' mental health and attempting to reduce any associated stigma. You can ensure an employee with mental illness feels supported by:

> **Talking with employees.** You recognize that having a secret at work and not getting the help he needs, can cause stress for an employee. As supervisor, you can encourage all employees to confide in you regarding their personal health and accommodation requirements. You recognize that you may never understand what it feels like to have a mental illness, but you commit to support employees in terms of the work they are given and any time off that is needed for them to tend to an illness. You can be understanding, and reduce the stigma, by making sure an employee doesn't feel ashamed. In addition, you can be supportive through the language you use; saying that she *is dealing with* an illness is more positive than saying she *suffers* from an illness.

Organizational Culture (PF2) includes being fair with employees and building trust. This can be difficult as you attempt to accommodate employees' stress management styles and mental illnesses with different work arrangements. When an employee confides in you and requests accommodations, you must keep that information private. When other employees see that someone is getting special treatment, they may feel they are being treated unfairly. You can increase your chances of being seen as fair in these types of situations by:

Building trust. As supervisor, you can be open with what the accommodations look like, that is, what is going to be happening, and ask for the other employees to cooperate. You have to be very careful not to disclose reasons for the accommodation, but ask employees to trust that you are doing the right thing, and let them know that if they needed help you would do what you could for them as well. Ensure that you are not treating employees unfairly by overloading them in an attempt to accommodate one individual; you don't want to take stress away from one person and add it to another. The relationships you have built are going to help you at this time—are you beginning to see the WIIFM in *MeYouQ*?

Psychological Competencies & Requirements (PF5) involves matching an employee to the type of work he is able to handle. Different work situations require different interpersonal and emotional competencies. When you consider the strengths and weaknesses of your employees, you can place a person in a position that suits their strengths; if this is not possible, you might rotate employees through the positions and have them each share a little of the stress. You can better allocate your staff by:

Knowing your employees. As supervisor, you should be familiar with the skills and competencies of your employees, as well as their work preferences. As much as possible, when workforce planning, you can move people into positions where they are more likely to thrive. If you are not proactive in placing employees into suitable positions, you may end up hiring new people for the jobs that your existing people want, and that could be a stressor for many of them.

Workload Management (PF9) is about giving employees a reasonable workload. If your employees already have too much work to do, and feel you are piling more work on them, they may not be able to handle it and could experience strain. In addition, some employees may be better able to handle more work, and therefore tend to get asked to take on more responsibilities. This has the potential to overstress those individuals as well. You can ease the stress on an employee's workload by:

> **Talking about workload.** Ask your employees if they feel they have a reasonable workload for them and in comparison to others. As a supervisor, you may make the mistake of looking at someone's workload from your perspective, not theirs. It doesn't matter whether you think something is fair, it matters what your employees' truths are. Be open in your conversations about workload, work to understand how people feel about their circumstances, and make adjustments where possible.

Are you aware of your own feelings of equality in the workplace? Write an example of how you felt you were being given less than someone else, or thought you deserved more. ___

_____

_____

Write an example of how you were given more than someone else, who might have also been deserving. _____

_____

_____

> **Chapter 22 Takeaways:**
> ↗ Different things cause stress in different people
> ↗ Each person has different strategies (moderators) for dealing with stress
> ↗ Stress can be motivating or debilitating; if not handled effectively, the person may experience strain and require medical attention
> ↗ Applications for Psychological Health and Safety include: being supportive, building trust, knowing your employees, and talking to

There are various strategies you can use to help your employees identify and manage stress. Good leadership skills are essential for having employees accept help from you with stress management and other skills. You can use various leadership theories to develop your own leadership style.

Chapter 23: Leadership

What kind of leader do you want to be?

TAKE ANY COURSE IN MANAGEMENT and you'll learn about leadership theories. The first group of theories said that leaders were born, not made. For a person to be a leader, he had to have certain traits, like being tall, or extroverted. Later theories said that leaders exhibited specific attributes, such as self-confidence and emotional intelligence. Trait theories moved from traits a person was born with to those that could be developed. While "born leaders" may have some characteristics that help them to succeed, leadership skills can generally be learned.

The next group of theories said it wasn't so much about the traits a person had, it was how they behaved that would make them a leader. For instance, a good leader may consult with employees, and allow them some input before making a decision. These types of people-related behaviors would lead to employee satisfaction and motivation. Theorists began to realize a leader's behavior had an impact on employees, and thought that a leader with the right type of behavior should be hired for the specific situation. This evolved into the recognition that a leader could, and should, choose the appropriate behavior for the particular situation.

Contingency theories said leaders should adjust their behavior to what followers need at a particular time; style is contingent on the situation. The selected style could be based upon the willingness and readiness of followers, as well as how much direction and leadership they need at a particular time, in a particular situation. The result will be a certain mix of task and relationship behavior styles. If an employee has a poor attitude, or doesn't know how to do the work, the leader will focus on styles related to task behavior. When a person can do the work, but isn't motivated, styles regarding relationship behavior will be appropriate. Employees who are motivated to work and can do the job will require very little leadership at all. There are lessons here to be remembered: adjust the level of direct supervision, the amount of support offered, and the level of employee participation to what is appropriate for the circumstance.

Motivation theories drove the next group of leadership philosophies, and stated that leaders needed to make a transaction with followers via what motivates them—reward, such as praise, or punishment, such as a reprimand. This type of leadership gets people to comply and do their jobs, but it doesn't do anything to inspire or engage people at work.

The latest iteration of leadership theories says that leaders transform people and workplaces. A transformational leader is someone who is charismatic and inspires followers with a vision. People will choose to follow a transformational leader, whether or not they have actual authority. This type of leader appeals to employees' intrinsic needs and serves as an important role model.

One goal of this book is to have you work towards being a positive influence on the lives of those around you; to develop a vision and inspire your employees. You are a unique individual, and you will have to develop your own leadership style. This leadership style will be something you are comfortable with, but it will also be what is necessary for the situation. Your style will grow out of conscious reflection, self-exploration, and trial and error, as you practice good human relations; it will become a conscious choice as you get to know yourself better and work to relate to others.

Think about this as you move into your new role. Get to know yourself better, and picture how your characteristics are going to fit into your work situation. Take some time during your transition to be conscious about the style you are going to use. Think about what is going to be effective with this particular group of employees. Work to understand each person, how their personal characteristics impact what they do, and how they relate to others.

Establish a positive working relationship with each employee and help them to have a positive relationship with each other. As you have built your *MeYouQ*, you can help others to build theirs as well. Work to have people like and respect you, not fear you. Work to have people respect and build empathy for each other. Remember it will take some time to build relationships with people; you can't rush rapport.

Write down the leadership characteristics that you have seen in others and would like to emulate. _____

_____

_____

Think of two places you have worked. Describe how leading the people in the first place would be different from leading the people in the second. _____

_____

_____

_____

_____

Your leadership style also has to function within the context of the organization you are working for. Embrace the vision, mission, and core values of the company, and work toward fulfilling them. The vision is the end goal of the company, for example: "A world where every supervisor is an effective one." The mission includes specific things the organization hopes to achieve, for example: "To develop skills for building psychologically healthy and safe workplaces." Core values are enduring beliefs that guide behavior, for example: "Be positive, and treat people well."

Just as the organization lives its vision, mission, and values, you live yours as a person. Take some time to define your personal vision, mission, and values, and adopt them in your role as supervisor. Think about how you can achieve these things within the context of the organization, how they pair together.

You will be highly motivated and engaged when you can see that your efforts are achieving these higher purposes.

Write out your personal vision, mission, and values. This should be the big picture for your life right now. _____

_____

_____

_____

_____

Applications for Employee Mental Health

Good leadership is especially important for Psychological Factors 2, 3, 4, 8, and 10.

Positive Organizational Culture (PF2) is possible when people in the organization trust each other. As a transformational leader you will be model trust by:

Maintaining consistent behavior. Employees need to be able to approach you and not worry about how you will react. Supervisors who are happy one moment, and stressed out the next, may scare employees away from bringing important information forward.

Doing what you say you'll do. Employees are going to be coming to you with requests for various things. When you commit to them that you are going to do something, it is important to follow through. If you fail to do so, they won't believe you the next time, or be interested in any new initiative you discuss.

Being transparent with decisions. Nothing stresses people out more, or starts the rumor mill faster, than suspicion. When staff members aren't given reasons for why one employee appears to be getting special treatment, or how the workloads were decided, they make up their own stories, and trust disappears. Being transparent means sharing your criteria and giving explanations for your decisions, without breaking privacy and confidentiality, of course.

Treating people with fairness. An employee wants to know he can come to work and be treated fairly each day. It's important to be respectful of a person's right to be free from discrimination and not to play favorites. In determining fairness, employees will assess how they are treated compared to: 1) their own standard of fairness and 2) how others are being treated. Remember, it doesn't matter if you think you are being fair, you need to deal with employee perceptions of the situation. Spend more time listening than defending your actions.

Being consistent in your message. When a supervisor says one thing to one employee, and something else to another, word will get around and trust will break down. It's also not fair that some employees have access to more details in a situation than others. Be careful what you are sharing with employees, and ensure your story doesn't change based on who you are talking to. If you have ideas you would like feedback on, perhaps asking another manager is a better idea than consulting one of your employees.

> **Have you ever mistrusted your manager? What did he or she do that made you feel this way? Or maybe you completely trust your manager. What makes you feel this way?** _____
>
> _____
>
> _____

Clear Leadership & Expectations (PF3) means employees know what is expected of them and what their roles are in the organization. Clarity is achieved by:

Setting a vision for the department. People want to be part of something larger than themselves. They want to know that what they are doing is important. These two things are achieved by articulating a vision for employees to follow. Ideally, the supervisor should embrace the organization's vision and use it as direction for the department.

Thinking before speaking. People will remember what you said, not what you meant to say. Think about how your remarks will be received and whether you might want to choose different words. Communicating by e-mail or text message is particularly tricky, so be sure to think about the different ways someone could interpret what you are sending.

Making a decision after careful analysis. Employees will distrust a supervisor who keeps changing the plan after a decision has been announced. Before unveiling your ideas, ensure you have done your due diligence and performed a proper analysis. Sometimes this will mean you ask for more time to think about something, but that is better than making a poor decision and having to change your mind later.

> **Does your manager make decisions without really thinking them through? What effect does that have? Or maybe your manager sets the vision for the department and is unwavering with decisions. How does this affect employees?** _____
>
> _____
>
> _____

Civility & Respect (PF4) will occur when people treat each other well. As employees are looking to you, their leader, as a role model, ensure you are:

Modeling inclusive behavior. Work to build a community in your department where everyone is included. Give all employees equal attention and do your best to intervene when exclusive groups start to form. When people get together after work, encourage them to include everyone.

Encouraging employees to relate positively to each other. As you have grown to know your employees better, you can bridge the gap between people by showing them the things they have in common with each other. Work to build *MeYouQ* skills in your employees.

Intervening when people aren't being treated fairly. When it comes to your attention that someone has been left out or ridiculed, step in and remedy the situation. Set expectations for behavior and coach individuals in *MeYouQ* as necessary. Be ready to explain why there needs to be civility and respect in the workplace. Organizations may have a respectful workplace policy to lean on if needed.

Do there seem to be in-groups and out-groups in your workplace? Have managers done anything to discourage this? What could/do they do? _____

_____

_____

_____

_____

Involvement & Influence (PF8) is inherent in the type of leadership style you form, and hopefully you have chosen a style where employees have some say in the things that affect them. People have a need to exercise some control over their own lives; you can help them do this by:

Empowering individuals. Employees feel powerless and demoralized when they have to go to the boss for permission on every little thing. Give them opportunities to make decisions, and show them how to approach the challenge. Allow them some leeway to try to solve their own problems and be supportive in their learning. If they initially fail, encourage them to keep trying. Give them the feedback they need to do a better job next time; be positive.

Allowing employee participation. It can be frustrating to feel as though you have no control over what happens to you, and this is also true at work. When something is going to affect employees, it may be appropriate to allow them to participate in the decision. Be careful not to ask for their ideas if you already have your mind made up, and ensure they know that you still have the final say. Your employees' insight can be very different from your own, and it could be a very important perspective to gain.

Sharing important information. When a change is in the works, people want to know what's going on. Distrust begins to creep in, and rumors begin to spread when employees aren't given any information. While you may not have much information to share at first, let them know what you are able to share, and reassure them that when you have something concrete to tell them, you will. Good change management practices are discussed in Chapter 29.

Does your manager solicit employee input? Is that input used? How does this make employees feel? _____

_____

_____

Engagement (PF10) requires the supervisor to help employees feel connected to their work so they will be motivated to do their job well. As a leader, you can enhance employee engagement by:

Showing employees their impact. Employees want to see how their efforts are helping the organization to achieve its goals. Work to link individual contributions to the achievement of the mission. When employees see the impact they are having on organizational success, they will be motivated to continue their efforts in the right direction.

Do you know your organization's mission statement? What are you doing in your job right now to contribute to it? _____

_____

_____

_____

_____

Chapter 23 Takeaways:

↗ Individuals must develop their own, authentic leadership style, while focusing on what employees need from their leaders

↗ Leaders must embrace the organization's vision, mission, and values

↗ Applications for Psychological Health and Safety include: being consistent in your behavior, doing what you say you'll do, being transparent with your actions, treating people with fairness, being consistent in your message, setting a vision for the department, thinking before speaking, making a decision after careful analysis, modeling inclusive behavior, encouraging employees to relate positively to each other, intervening when people aren't treated fairly, empowering individuals, allowing employee participation, sharing important information, and showing employees their impact

Having your own leadership style will help you live your purpose as your authentic self. When you combine that with effective personal management skills, you will serve as a model for others to use in developing their professional, authentic selves.

Chapter 24: Personal Management Tools

How many productivity tools do you use each day?

SEVERAL STRATEGIES ARE AVAILABLE to you and your employees to get your work done efficiently and effectively; these include time management, focusing, goal setting, prioritizing, and delegating. When everyone can get the work done on time, it will relieve the stress of people waiting on others to do their jobs, and it will ensure that everyone is doing his or her fair share of the work.

Time management. The chances are good that you are already able to manage your time. After all, people who can't handle their work are usually not promoted to supervisor. You may find, though, that the increase in your workload requires a little more attention to how you will manage your time. You may also find you have employees who need to develop their time management skills so they can handle their workloads effectively.

Good time management means you are making decisions about where to allocate your time. To do this, you have to know where your time is going; that is, how much time things take and what you are wasting your time on. When you know how long it takes you to do a certain activity, you can better plan your day and account for all the things that need to be done. When you are conscious about how much time you are wasting, you can avoid those activities and make better use of your time.

Typical time-wasters include: allowing others to use up your time unnecessarily, spending too much time on technology and relaxation, and fixing mistakes that you could have avoided if you took the time to plan your activity before beginning. Strategies available for dealing with these time-wasters include: letting people know you don't have time to talk right now, setting your cell phone or email aside, having all the materials available before you begin your task, taking a refresher break so you will be able to concentrate, measuring twice and cutting once, and leaving for work early so you aren't stuck in traffic. Any problem can be solved, but you have to define it first. Most people aren't able to see how all of the little time-wasters throughout the day add up to negatively impact their productivity.

Track your time over a few days. What kinds of things waste your time? _____

_____

_____

_____

What can you do, specifically, to reduce the time that is being wasted? _____

_____

_____

Focusing. As much as you manage your own time, you may experience disruptions that you can't control. When this happens, are you able to get back to what you were doing quickly, or does it take you a while to pick up where you left off? When the room is noisy, are you able to block out the noise and concentrate on the task at hand?

While it may feel like you can't change your environment, you may be able to grab a little bit of control in a particular situation. You might block out time to be uninterrupted, or ask people to schedule an appointment with you for non-urgent matters. You can mark your spot in your work, or write yourself a reminder, and force yourself to get right back on task after your disruption. You can use a notepad to jot down additional activities or ideas that come up while you are working on something else, so you don't worry about forgetting something important. You can ask visitors to talk with you about non-work related activities during lunch or break. You can remain standing for a quick chat, so the visitor doesn't get too comfortable and stay longer than necessary.

If you find you just can't focus, it might be that you need a break. Make sure you don't schedule yourself so tightly that you can't take a bit of time to refresh from a difficult task. Rewarding yourself for focusing on and completing a task might also be a good idea. Maybe that coffee break has to wait until you're done!

What distracts you, or causes you to lose focus? _____

_____

_____

What can you do to stop the distraction, or minimize the disruption? _____

_____

_____

Goal setting. If you feel as though you are getting nothing accomplished, it could be because you haven't defined what is important for you to achieve; you haven't decided what you need to spend your time on. It could also mean that you are procrastinating because you find the task unpleasant or uninteresting. Setting SMART goals is commonly recommended. Your goals should be specific, measurable, attainable, realistic, and time-deadlined.

Your goals should be specific enough to define what you are working on; that is, the scope of the task. This will help you to outline all of the smaller tasks that are necessary to undertake in the pursuit of the goal, and will allow you to gauge how much time it will take.

Goals should be measurable, so you know when you are done. The measurement must be applicable to the type of goal, and could be something like completing it by a certain time, to a certain level of performance, with a level of quality in mind, or to a level of completion.

Goal attainability means you won't set goals that you are not capable of achieving or don't have the resources to complete. While it is important to push yourself and set challenging goals, frustration can discourage the pursuit of goals when you lack ability, or resources are not falling into place.

A realistic goal would be one that is doable in terms of the other goals you may have. While you might be capable and have the resources, are there too many other demands on your time to be able to take on something else right now?

Setting a time-deadline for the goal is critical. You could have the best of intentions to pursue a goal, but if there is no sense of urgency or time pressure, you may never set it as a priority. It is not enough to set a goal; you must have the motivation to work on it.

Setting SMART goals can help you to gain perspective on all the things you want to and need to do. You may find that something you thought you wanted to do isn't something you want to do anymore. You may also find that something you want to do becomes better defined and moves within your reach when you have a realistic picture of what's involved.

Write a SMART goal for something you want to do. _____

_____

_____

_____

_____

What's the first step you need to take toward achieving this goal?

_____

_____

Ok, go get started!

Prioritizing. Your goals will have a list of daily, weekly, and monthly tasks associated with them. How do you know what to work on at any given time? Many people prioritize in their minds, but you may find that your job as supervisor has many more tasks than you are used to. Not only are you expected to prioritize your own tasks, you need to be concerned with those of the whole team.

The first step in prioritizing is to make a task list; look at what needs to get done in the next few days and the next few weeks. Write out your task list in just enough detail that you know what you must do; it's not necessary to include every single move you have to make.

Once you have your to-do list, scour the list for the items that _must_ get done today, the items that _should_ get done today, and the items that would be _nice_ to get done today, if you have extra time.

You can create your list of priorities for tomorrow at the end of today, but when you arrive at work tomorrow, you should make sure nothing has changed that affects your priorities. Work on your "must do" tasks first, even if they are not your favorite things to do.

Your task list will have some things that can be delegated to others, and some things that are no longer relevant and can be removed from the list. Many managers are reluctant to delegate, but being able to delegate effectively can increase your department's capabilities.

> **What is something you must do in the next couple of days? Have you been avoiding it? How will you make sure it gets done?**
>
> _____
>
> _____
>
> _____

Delegating. Employees want to be given the opportunity to be trusted with important tasks. Supervisors may be reluctant to delegate these tasks to them, for fear they won't get done properly. By investing time now to train employees on these tasks, the supervisor will save time later because the employee will be able to handle it on their own.

Delegating means giving someone the authority and responsibility to complete the task, but ultimate responsibility rests with the supervisor. If the task is not done properly, or on time, the blame cannot be shifted to the employee. To delegate effectively you have to: choose the right person, train him on the new task, set the expectations for performance, give him the opportunity to practice, let him know that it's ok to make mistakes and ask for help, maintain contact with him throughout execution of the task, and use positive feedback when he succeeds. Be careful not to delegate important decisions that you should be making. Also ensure you offer different employees these opportunities.

What is something you can delegate to an employee? _____

_____

Do you have enough time to support the delegation effectively?

_____

Who might be interested in the growth opportunity and be able to handle it? _____

What would you have to do to prepare this person to take on the task? _____

_____

Some people are better than others with time management, focusing, setting goals, and prioritizing. Recognize that your employees may seem like they are shirking their responsibilities, but they may just need to develop better personal management tools. Instead of getting upset with people for being disorganized and not getting their work done, work with them to find the problem and develop better personal management abilities.

Don't give them too many different things to work on at once, as old habits may be tough to break.

Perhaps you cannot understand why someone is procrastinating when the task is interesting. While it's true the task may be interesting to them, perhaps they don't know how to do it or where to start. Don't make assumptions; communicate with your employees to see why they do what they do. When you understand your employees better, you can work with them more effectively and resolve situations without harming relationships.

Which of your employees might have some personal management skill issues? _____

What will you say to him or her to show support and that you want to help? _____

_____

Applications for Employee Mental Health

Good personal management skills are important for Psychological Factors 4, 6, 9, 10, and 11.

Civility & Respect (PF4) involves people being courteous in their interactions with others at work. You can encourage respectfulness in the workplace by:

Ensuring everyone does their fair share. When an employee is able to manage his time, know the priorities, and work on goals, he will achieve better performance. Not only will his own productivity be better, his co-workers will feel a sense of equality. A person may feel a sense of inequity when she compares the rewards she earns for her efforts to the rewards others are getting for their efforts. If an employee feels that she is not getting enough or someone else is getting too much, she may try to restore equity by reducing her efforts, asking for more rewards, pressuring others to increase their efforts, or even quitting to go to another job. When employees each do their fair share, this is less likely to happen. People will feel there is equity in the workplace. You can ensure people have goals to work on and are working diligently to facilitate this feeling.

Reminding everyone to respect each other's time. When an employee isn't doing her fair share that's one thing, but when she is going around visiting and distracting others, that's disrupting. By training employees on how to manage time and focus better, they will become aware of distractors and time-wasters and will come to realize that they might be someone else's distractor. Use positive reinforcement to encourage people to work hard and achieve goals, and remind distracted people of what they need to be focusing on.

Sharing reasons for delegating. Part of delegating is being transparent in your actions. To avoid looking like you are playing favorites and causing jealousy among employees, you can announce that a certain employee will be taking on a special project, and that you expect the rest of the team to be supportive by sharing information or covering some of his regular duties as required. You can let people know that there will be opportunities for other staff members to participate in these types of projects in the future, and be prepared to follow through.

Growth & Development (PF6) occurs when the supervisor takes the time to show employees how to do their jobs properly. You can encourage growth and development by:

Teaching personal management tools. You shouldn't only focus on the technical job tasks (hard skills), but on the soft skills as well. The personal management skills an employee learns will help him to take on challenges and be confident that he can be effective on the job. Soft skills are transferrable to a variety of situations, so you never know how a person will benefit from these skills in the future. A little work coaching someone may be beneficial now and even more so in the future.

Delegating important tasks. Select the jobs for delegation that can be beneficial to a person's growth. Be careful not to delegate only the jobs that you find unpleasant. If you know what a person's career aspirations are, you can better match the task to the individual. Let her know this is a skill she needs for the future and she will be motivated! If you aren't in touch with people's interests and abilities, you won't be able to make the most out of these situations.

Workload Management (PF9) means ensuring employees have enough time to complete the tasks required of them. It might not be that they have too many tasks, it might just be that they are wasting too much time or don't have a clear direction to move in. As supervisor, you can help them with their time management by:

Teaching time management skills. When an employee complains she can't get her work done, first diagnose the cause. Does she have the skills to do the job, is the amount of work you are asking her to do unreasonable, or is there some other barrier to her performance? Check to see that she is using her time effectively. If you aren't sure, ask her to track what she is spending her time on each day. Help her to locate those activities that are time-wasters. Maybe she is spending too much time walking back and forth to get things, and she should use one trip. Maybe she is procrastinating because of lack of motivation, or she doesn't know where to start. Once you find the problem, you can figure out a solution.

Helping employees focus. Is your employee in a position where disruptions from customers or co-workers are common? You might not be able to stop the interruptions, but you can teach her how to get back to work more quickly after being disrupted, and encourage her to develop her own strategies for doing so. Maybe she has to mark her spot, or make a note to do something later; whatever is it, get her to train her mind to block out distracting thoughts and return to them later.

Working on goal setting. A person who feels his workload is too heavy might be trying to do too much. Perhaps some things are required for his job, while others are his own ideas of what should be done. In project management, you are supposed to write a scope statement, which outlines the parameters of the project. The tendency of people working on a project is to keep adding on nice-to-have extras that are not part of the original plan. He can remain on track by using the project scope statement to determine whether he should be working on something or not. Similarly, he can use a set of goals to ensure that what he is working on is required to achieve the end result; anything not related to a specific goal should be eliminated.

Helping them prioritize tasks. Each employee has his favorite things to do at work. He might gravitate to those tasks first, at the expense of a task that needs to be done sooner. When he realizes that something else is due right away, he might stress out about not having enough time. Train your employee to make a task list and do the ones that are most important or most urgent first. When those tasks are completed, he can move to the important but not urgent ones; then to the unimportant, nice-to-do tasks. Another important thing to consider when looking at the task list is interdependencies. If someone is waiting on him to finish a task so she can do hers, that task should have priority. He should be able to choose the right tasks to work on at any given time. Make sure he knows the big picture in terms of the work that needs to be done.

Engagement (PF10) means an employee is connected to her work, motivated to do her job well, and has the personal management skills necessary to achieve her optimal performance. As a supervisor, you can enhance employee engagement by:

Increasing discretionary time. You hope employees will be engaged in their work because if they are, they will go beyond their regular duties and use their discretionary time to benefit your organization. However, without good personal management practices, there may be little, if any, time left over. Encourage employees to manage themselves well, and they will have extra time to contribute to the tasks that feed their passion and values.

Setting challenging goals. When using the SMART goal system with your employees, make sure they set attainable, yet challenging goals. A more difficult goal will bring more personal satisfaction, and employees will be more excited to work on tasks that give them intrinsic value. Encourage employees to reach a little higher, and give them the support they need to get there. If the goals appear to be too high, help them to set smaller goals and have some victories first, before they attempt something more difficult.

Prioritizing development activities. An employee may already be engaged and have many things she is interested in doing in the workplace. She might like to undertake a new project, sit on committees, or plan special events, for example. If your employee was to pursue all of these activities at once, it's likely she would burn out from overextending herself.

Talk with your employee about her ideas and remind her about what a reasonable workload would be. Get her to prioritize which projects she wants to, or should, work on now, in terms of her overall career goals and the needs of the organization. In this way, she can remain focused and motivated until the project is done and she is ready to move on to the next challenge.

Balance (PF11) involves looking at the demands on an employee in terms of their home, work, and personal lives. Personal management skills can be transferred to one's life outside of work as well. As a supervisor, you assist an employee's work-life balance by:

Encouraging further use of skills. When it appears an employee is having trouble with work-life balance, talk to him about all of his obligations. If he appears to have too many things to handle, encourage him to prioritize. If he suggests that he has no energy to do anything when he gets home after work, perhaps a little personal goal setting will provide the motivation. It's important to encourage a person to plan some downtime as well; some mindless activity will help him rest, so he can get geared up to work hard again. See the employee as a whole person, who has to play and manage a variety of roles.

Showing interest in personal goals. Get to know your employees somewhat on a personal level. Ask them about plans they have, or activities they are involved in outside of work. It's not to pry, it's to show a genuine interest in people, and to show you care. When an employee feels you care, it will be easier for her to be away from home and feel good about contributing at work. When people are able to talk about their personal dreams at work they will feel like a whole person, not divided or disconnected.

Giving employees some control. Employers are more frequently being asked to be flexible with work schedules when there are family obligations to take care of. Giving an employee some control over how he spends his time will help him to manage his work and family responsibilities in a manner that works for him. That's not to say that you need to give him control over his whole schedule, or let him miss excessive time from the office, but control over part of his time may make the difference between success and failure in all his duties.

Allowing employees to unplug. If organizations expect their employees to be available by cell phone during their off-work hours, they could be putting unfair demands on their time. When possible, encourage your employees to shut down from work at the end of the day. Let them know it is ok to answer e-mail and phone messages the next day; in fact, insist they do.

What personal management tricks and tips do you have that you can share with an employee? _____

_____

_____

_____

_____

_____

_____

_____

_____

_____

_____

_____

Think of a person who appears disorganized in your workplace. What do you think the problem is? _____

_____

As the supervisor, what would you say to help him or her? Write a short script. _____

_____

_____

_____

_____

Chapter 24 Takeaways:

↗ To manage time well, you need to recognize time-wasters and control where your time is spent

↗ Supervisors can have many interruptions during the workday; you need to develop strategies for regaining focus on tasks

↗ Setting goals is important for productivity; SMART goals are suggested

↗ Task lists are useful; some tasks can be delegated as development opportunities for employees, though you remain accountable

↗ It is important to know what your most important task is at any given time; remember the priority of tasks can change quickly

↗ Applications for Psychological Health and Safety include: ensuring everyone does their fair share, reminding everyone to respect each other's time, sharing reasons for delegating, teaching personal management tools, delegating important tasks, teaching time management skills, helping employees focus, working on goal setting, helping employees prioritize tasks, increasing discretionary time, setting challenging goals, prioritizing developmental activities, encouraging further use of skills, showing interest in personal goals, giving employees some control, and allowing employees to unplug

When you take the time to develop your employees' personal management skills, you will have more faith that the work you are asking them to do will be done efficiently. It is important to use professional techniques when you direct the work of others.

Chapter 25: Directing the Work of Others

Do people willingly do things for you when you ask them?

ALL EYES ARE ON THE SUPERVISOR, and any slip up in what you say or do can leave a lasting impression on your employees. An employee can take something you say, or do, the wrong way and quickly lose respect for you. When directing the work of others, it is important to be able to use an appropriate communication style, exhibit positive behavior, and withstand criticism.

Appropriate communication style. Your verbal and nonverbal communication styles can impact your ability to communicate effectively with employees. Good verbal communication could mean using "I" language to say what you mean, providing the appropriate amount of information for the individual, or using professional language. Good nonverbal communication includes watching the tone in your voice, and ensuring you aren't doing anything with your eyes, face, or body that would send the wrong message.

These communication styles are especially important when you are trying to gain cooperation from employees while directing their work. For instance, you might be inclined to ask a staff member if they "would mind" doing something, allowing them the option of saying they do mind. Instead of approaching it with a question where they have the choice to refuse, issue polite commands such as, "Please stock the shelves now." Remember to say, "Thank you," when employees do what you ask.

Paying attention to what you are saying is also important. Of course a supervisor should not be engaging in gossip, rumors, or negative talk about the organization or its employees, but even trivial things said jokingly can negatively impact your employees. Sarcasm, or "harmless" little comments can be confusing to people, or taken personally. As much as possible, you should refrain from saying anything that could be taken the wrong way. Also consider self-fulfilling prophecy; if you say an employee is not a good worker, you will treat him that way and he will never aspire to be better. If you think of him as valuable and treat him that way, he will strive to become an even greater asset.

When issuing a directive, you want to make sure the person is going to comply and do the task the way you asked. Involve her in the conversation and check for understanding. Say, "Just so I know we're talking about the same thing, can you please walk me through what you are going to do now?" This will close the communication feedback loop and you can correct any misconceptions early on (recall the communication model from Chapter 15).

Another potential for a communication problem is your reaction to bad news, such as someone making a mistake, or something not being ready on time. If you choose to react in anger and yell at people, they are not going to come to you with a problem in the future. People should not be afraid to be honest with you. A better reaction to bad news would be to remain calm, ask appropriate questions, and figure out how to solve the problem. Allowing people to learn from their mistakes is a great step in their development, and you should support them by being patient in these situations.

Think of two things you would have to ask an employee to do. How would you ask in a manner that is likely to gain cooperation? _____

_____

_____

_____

_____

In your examples, are you making any assumptions about what the employee knows or doesn't know? What information might he or she need in order to comply? _____

_____

_____

Appropriate behavior. In the leadership section, you saw the importance of being consistent in your behavior. This section will look at behaving in a fun, positive, helpful way, while treating others fairly. Your conduct sets the tone for behavior in the department. If you work hard, others will too. People will watch the way you interact with others and use that as a model for their own interactions.

Do you think it's ok to have fun at work? It's important for employees to enjoy what they do. They can enjoy the challenge of the work and the tasks they are doing, but to enjoy the organization and the people they work with requires having a bit of fun. It's ok to be a little playful with employees and not take yourself so seriously, as long as you maintain professional boundaries. Make sure your fun is not at the expense of others, and that everyone is included when there's fun to be had. The positive feelings generated from having fun will improve moods and impact customers and clients as well. Of course you won't let employees forget that there is still work to be done.

Maintaining a positive attitude is not just about having fun. It's also about avoiding negativity. The idea is that a negative, pessimistic attitude can wear on people and add to their stress. Too much complaining or only seeing the downside to things does not make people feel good. Even when something unfortunate happens, work to see the bright side, or at least the realistic one.

Helping others is an important behavior to model. When there's lots of work to be done, employees will appreciate it if you roll up your sleeves and help them out. Your assistance will set the tone for them to help each other as well, whether or not you are around. When people are willing to help, more people will be willing to ask for help. This can mean that important work is getting done properly and on time. Be sure to offer assistance to everyone, so that everyone has the opportunity for success, regardless of gender or any other characteristic.

Employees will also appreciate it when they see you working hard at your own job. When you are getting things done and following up with them, they will have confidence in you. Your strong work ethic will set a standard for their performance. If you work hard they know you expect them to work hard. Of course, the opposite is true as well. If you are lazy in your job, they will have the tendency to be the same, as they are following the example you have set.

What have you done to show positivity at work lately? _____

_____

_____

What kinds of things can you do to help your employees? _____

_____

_____

_____

Withstand criticism. The ability to grow a thick skin is important, as you may have some employees who are overly critical of you. A thick skin means that you don't take comments personally and you don't become easily offended. You are able to withstand negativity and judgment, and remain objective and caring. Sounds easy, doesn't it? Probably not.

One thing you can do to withstand criticism is realize that people act on perceptions, not reality. It may not matter what you intended to do or say, it only matters how someone interprets it. Recall that you cannot argue with someone that her perception is not reality; her perception is her reality. You have to deal with her perception. For example, if an employee thinks you are treating her unfairly, don't argue the point with her. Talk about why she feels that way and work to see her point of view. Know what the problem is before you try to solve it, and work to clear up any misconceptions.

Another thing you can do to withstand criticism is recognize that the employee may have a point in his comments about you. If you can take what he said and pick out the constructive criticism from the destructive criticism, you might be able to agree that there's something you could have done differently in the situation. Some people don't communicate well; try not to worry too much about how they said something, but look at what they were trying to say. You can see that between this lesson and the one in the last paragraph, you are going to have to choose the path of doing what's right and not lower yourself to their level, another example of "taking the high road."

Finally, to withstand criticism, you can take the view that everyone is entitled to his or her opinion, and you don't have to agree. You can listen to what was said, see if you agree, and decide to not accept the feedback, if you think that's what's best for you. Listen, and thank them for their input. If it's appropriate, explain why you are going to continue to do things your way. If it's not appropriate to comment, just drop it like it never happened.

What have you been criticized for lately? How did you handle it?

_____

_____

_____

What could you have done to be more accepting of someone else's opinion? _____

_____

_____

Taking the time to ensure you are communicating with your employees' needs in mind shows empathy. Work to recognize how your own style might be affecting your ability to communicate; for example, facial expressions you may inadvertently use when you are trying to understand something, or becoming distracted during a conversation. When you become more aware in these ways, you will be able to choose the appropriate action for the situation.

Being positive, and having fun with employees shows that you care for them. It shows that you aren't just task-oriented; you value your relationships with them as well. From a *MeYouQ* perspective, recognize that what you find fun may not be what they find fun. Test out a few ideas to see what works, and make sure everyone is included.

Remember that your employees may not have good self-awareness or self-management skills in terms of how they think and talk about their work. Forgive them. Value and care for them even when you disagree. Try to understand where they are coming from, remain objective and caring, and be able to separate the person from the problem. Deal with the situation effectively, without allowing it to affect how you feel about that person; avoid holding a grudge, or allowing your feelings to build to a point where you are resentful.

Applications for Employee Mental Health

Using positive techniques to direct the work of others is important for Psychological Factors 1, 2, 3, 6, and 12.

Psychological Support (PF1) can be made possible through your appropriate means of communicating and possessing an attitude of helping others. When an employee comes to you to discuss a difficult situation regarding her mental health or stress levels, you can show psychological support by:

Responding positively. When an employee brings an illness or issue to your attention, be able to listen with understanding and not judgment. Engage with the employee in the type of conversation that is needed to support him or her. Using a caring tone of voice, proper body language, and careful selection of words is important at this time.

Offering to help. Once you are aware of the situation, you can work to accommodate any special needs. It's important an employee not have to worry about his job security while he deals with an illness. Involve the employee in the solution, giving him a choice where possible. Some work flexibility might make the difference between the person being able to deal effectively with an issue or not.

What would be your initial reaction if someone was having performance problems and used depression as an explanation? What would you say to show a positive response? _____

_____

_____

What kind of help could you offer in the context of your organization and the work your employees do? _____

_____

_____

_____

Organizational Culture (PF2) can be influenced by the supervisor through his or her use of desired communication practices and behaviors. The supervisor really does set the tone for workplace culture and what is considered acceptable behavior, whether it's through what he or she says about behavior, or how he or she models desired behavior. As a supervisor, you can positively influence organizational culture by:

Being honest. People in the workplace should be able to expect honesty from each other. By being able to withstand criticism and by not reacting poorly to bad news, you can encourage honesty. By using appropriate communication styles, you can be honest with employees and keep your relationships intact. If employees know they can ask for help when they need it, they will be honest about their needs.

Earning trust. Building a culture of helping others also fosters a caring atmosphere. When employees feel you care about them and their success, they will trust you with their futures. They will feel reassured that you have their best interests in mind. As employees learn to trust their leader, they will also learn to trust each other.

Valuing others. Having fun and being positive at work shows you are concerned with employees' minds and spirits. As a supervisor, you recognize that there is more to a person than just how much work you can get out of them. Keeping things light will help with their stress levels and overall satisfaction. If you are only task-oriented and pay no attention to relationships, people won't feel valued or satisfied.

Treating people fairly. Employees keep track of what they get compared to what others get, not just in terms of compensation, but also in attention and workloads. When employees see that you give equal assistance to everyone, they will feel there is equity at work. You will be able to maintain a positive, productive department by fostering this feeling, and hopefully they will treat others fairly as well.

> **Do you have the kind of organizational culture at work that you would like to have? If not, what specific actions can you begin to take to see a culture shift?** _____
>
> _____
>
> _____
>
> _____

Clear Leadership & Expectations (PF3) will be easier for you to accomplish as you pay more attention to how you are communicating with your employees. You will be able to give clear, understandable directions, and model the work ethic you expect. You can achieve clear leadership and expectations by:

Communicating fully. The different ways you communicate with employees impacts your ability to provide proper leadership. Paying attention to your verbal and nonverbal language will ensure you are giving a consistent message, without distractions or negative consequences, like offending someone. Being able to accept criticism will help you to see room for your own improvement; you can adjust your leadership style as needed. When you are able to accept bad news and talk to employees about it, you have the opportunity to clarify any misconceptions.

Ensuring cooperation. When you develop your own style of giving polite commands, and ensure they are being understood before work begins, you will be setting employees up for success at work. You should have fewer miscommunications and fewer situations where expectations were unclear. Because you are modeling appropriate behavior as well, people will respect you as their boss.

> **During your next conversation, pay attention to your nonverbal language. Is it distracting? Does it contradict the message you want to give? What should you be mindful to do (or not do) in future conversations?** _____
>
> _____
>
> _____
>
> _____

Growth & Development (PF6) activities are important for an employee to feel engaged in her work. When an employee is getting developmental attention from the supervisor, she is going to be motivated to work harder and to improve in a variety of areas. You can teach your employees to use appropriate communication and be able to take criticism. You can further aid in their development by:

Encouraging them to learn from mistakes. When you talk through mistakes fully, you are having the patience to encourage the employee to learn for next time. If you get upset when employees make a mistake, you may discourage them from trying new things. Using mistakes as a learning opportunity will give employees confidence to set higher goals, and achieve things they wouldn't otherwise try. When employees become proficient at their jobs, they will be in a position to make some decisions on their own. You can empower your employees to do this by giving them guidelines to use in making decisions, trusting them to do their best, and helping them to learn from their mistakes.

Expecting growth in interpersonal skills. Setting the tone for the department with your own behavior, and holding employees to that standard, will encourage them to look for ways to improve. When an employee is communicating inappropriately, exhibiting poor behavior, or criticizing others unfairly, you can take the opportunity to help them build their *MeYouQ*; the key for them to relate better to others is to first understand their own traits and behaviors. Your employees need to see how their multiple identities—race, family status, gender, etc.—are coming together to make them the person they are, and how they contribute to explain why they do what they do.

Think about someone you know who could use some development in soft skills. Do you have a trusting relationship with this person? Would he or she be accepting of your efforts to help? Plan how you are going to approach the situation. _____

_____

_____

_____

Psychological Protection (PF12) provides for employees' mental health in the workplace. The supervisor must ensure good communication and respect between employees, as well as with customers. Have a zero tolerance policy for unacceptable behaviors and criticism. Just because you are able to withstand criticism, it doesn't mean your employees are able to. You can protect your employees by:

Maintaining positivity. Your employees will feel more at ease as you control your reactions to stressful events and approach these situations with problem solving in mind. Instead of entertaining complaining by employees, encourage them to come up with solutions. Pay no attention when people are complaining for the sake of complaining, it's in some people's nature to complain.

Reinforcing appropriate behaviors. Instead of focusing on the things employees are doing wrong, let them know what they are doing right. The idea behind positive reinforcement is to reward employees for good behavior, with the intention of having the behavior repeated. Congratulate employees for appropriate behavior, and if they are doing something incorrectly, simply show them how to improve.

Using courtesy. As you are using polite commands to direct the work of employees, encourage others to do the same when they are working alongside their peers. Appropriate manners are important from customers as well. If a customer is not being courteous, step in to assist. Have policies in your department for how people are expected to treat each other. Many emergency rooms, for example, have had to hang signs regarding waiting room behavior to take the stress off the front-line staff.

Building emotional intelligence. Poor communication and behavior might be due to employees being unable to handle their emotions. Just as you can become aware of your emotions and work to manage how those emotions affect your behavior, you can help your employees do the same. When you notice an employee having an outburst at work, take the opportunity to teach him or her about emotional intelligence.

What has happened at work lately that could negatively affect employee mental health? How was it handled and how should it have been handled? _____

_____

_____

_____

_____

_____

_____

_____

_____

_____

_____

_____

Chapter 25 Takeaways:

↗ Pay attention to what you say to employees and how you say it, both verbally and nonverbally; be gentle when people make mistakes

↗ Gain cooperation by being direct and using polite commands; check that employees understand what is being asked of them

↗ Avoid gossip and sarcasm; use positive language and treat people as if they are competent and capable

↗ Model the behavior you want to see in employees; be hardworking and consistent in your own behavior

↗ Be positive, have a little fun, and help others

↗ Be able to withstand criticism; remember that someone's perception is their reality

↗ Take criticism objectively; improve where you can, and be willing to discuss differences

↗ Applications for Psychological Health and Safety include: responding positively, offering to help, being honest, earning trust, valuing others, treating people fairly, communicating fully, ensuring cooperation, encouraging learning from mistakes, expecting growth in interpersonal skills, maintaining positivity, reinforcing appropriate behaviors, using courtesy, and building emotional intelligence

Use caring and supportive methods for directing the work of your employees. If they are not functioning fully at their jobs, be patient and offer additional training for them to be successful.

Chapter 26: Training

Could your training methods be more effective?

A SUPERVISOR WILL HAVE TO TRAIN employees for one thing or another at some point. When you use proven techniques for training, you will assist your employees in learning quickly. Training is used for technical job skills, as well as in some common areas, in an effort to solve general workplace problems. In our service-oriented, knowledge-based organizations, it is important to build a culture of sharing information and valuing learning. These attitudes and actions will add to the human capital in your organization; your employees will have the skills they need for their current and future positions. To assist you in your training and learning responsibilities, this section will cover the job instruction method, diversity and ethics training, knowledge sharing in the organization, and building a culture of continuous learning.

Job instruction training. It is likely that you will give an employee on-the-job training, or teach someone else how to train a peer to do a new task. Using the job instruction training method is a useful approach to take, as the step-by-step instruction, explanations, and repetition are all useful for learning. Job instruction training looks like this:

1. Tell the trainee what you are going to be covering. Ascertain the trainee's previous experience with the type

of work or equipment. Put the learner at ease by making a connection to what he already knows, and telling him you are confident he will catch on quickly and be performing the task on his own in no time.

2. Place the trainee beside you, where he can see what you're doing. Ensure he is looking at the task from your vantage point. Demonstrate the task while explaining what you are doing, why you are doing it, and any important things he needs to know about safety when doing the job. Go slowly enough for him to follow.

3. Demonstrate the task a second time, but this time ask the trainee to explain what you are doing and why. Get him to dictate the step-by-step process. If he forgets to mention something, fill in the blanks for him and ensure he has complete information.

4. Turn the task over to the trainee. Have him perform the task, while explaining what he is doing and why, and paying attention to safety. Ensure nothing is forgotten.

5. For positive reinforcement, have him do the task once more while you question him on what he is doing and why.

6. Congratulate the trainee on learning the task, and offer yourself as a resource in the future if he needs you. Check in with the employee regularly for the first little while to make sure the job is going well and he has no questions.

A larger task might be a lot to learn at once. If you break the task into chunks to teach one at a time, make sure you present the smaller tasks in the same order they will be done when they are all brought back together. Have the employee demonstrate he can perform the entire task once the training is completed.

Is job instruction training different from what you've used before? If so, how? _____

_____

_____

_____

New employee orientation. The goals of a new employee orientation are to have the employee become productive quickly, and ensure she is comfortable with her surroundings; to make her feel like she fits in. When a new employee does not feel like part of the organization, she is not likely going to stay for more than a few weeks, to a few months. The supervisor plays an important role in the orientation (also called onboarding).

Some organizations provide online training to employees and collect their personal information even before the first day of work. This can be helpful in preparing to welcome the employee properly on the first day, and in not overwhelming her with paperwork and policies. The new hire will likely shadow an experienced employee on the job for the first little while, and this peer can use the job instruction method. That staff member, or another, may serve as a buddy for the employee, to show her around and introduce her to other people in the organization. During the orientation, the new employee needs to receive personal attention from the supervisor. If it's in the budget, she can be taken to lunch and time can be spent getting to know her better.

Orientation is not only for the first day of work, it can go on for days or even weeks. The supervisor needs to continue to play a key role during this time, and ensure the employee feels supported. Managers make a mistake when they simply hand the person off to others in the organization; they need to be available for a period of time and should be checking in regularly to see how things are going. Some organizations use a sheet of staff pictures and names to assist the new person in becoming familiar with her co-workers. Employees can take turns sitting with her at lunch and mentoring her in other aspects of the organization.

> **Think about a good orientation that you had. What did they do really well that you could implement?** _____
>
> _____
>
> _____
>
> _____

Diversity and anti-harassment training. You might have employee conflict in your organization because people are from different backgrounds, or because of the diverse groups which are represented. Diversity training is used to develop an awareness of differences and to change inappropriate behaviors.

Diversity awareness involves learning about another culture or group of people. When employees can understand each other better, they can appreciate each other as individuals. When differences become less foreign, they can be less scary and cause less discomfort. Diversity training may uncover differences in cultures, behaviors, or values, which may include whether the culture is individualistic, whether people are on time for appointments, how much formality and respect is shown to elders and superiors, whether talking about personal lives is expected before doing business, and if subordinates are usually allowed input into decisions. Diversity training about different groups, such as members of the LGBTTQ community, may involve cultivating an understanding about biological differences and the struggles people face.

When working with different cultures or populations, it is important to accept differences, but also to reach an agreement on how everyone is going to come together as a team. The idea is to allow some differences, so people can be themselves and feel comfortable in the workplace, while deciding where differences are not allowed. A group needs to work on ground rules, such as everyone has to be on time for meetings, everyone is going to be involved in decision making, and everyone must speak the same language in team meetings. Building acceptance doesn't mean employees simply tolerate others, it means they respect differences and don't require others to change who they are to be a member of the team. Sometimes, however, some people will need more than a little diversity education.

Some individuals not only have to change their attitudes, they have to change their behaviors. You may have an employee who does not appreciate differences and is outwardly hostile or rude, and you will have to conduct anti-harassment training. This type of training will present the organization's commitment to a harassment-free workplace, define unacceptable behavior, and outline the penalties that apply when someone is engaging in harassment. With respect to diverse cultures and groups, your harassment policy may demand that people keep comments and jokes to themselves, and that they not have any images, posted or visible, that would be degrading to someone else.

The organization is likely to have a policy on sexual harassment as well, which will require training. These policies reiterate the organization's commitment to providing a harassment-free workplace, define what is meant by sexual harassment, and outline the penalties that would apply to someone engaging in this type of harassment. Sexual harassment policies prohibit demanding sexual favors in exchange for job opportunities—called Quid Pro Quo harassment—as well as comments and images that create a hostile work environment.

Have you heard anyone tell a degrading joke lately? Did you laugh? What should you do instead? _____

_____

What should you say to someone who engaged in this type of behavior? _____

_____

_____

Ethics. Training in ethics may seem unnecessary if you believe most people have common sense. When you are working with people who have so many different personal experiences and multiple roles, you can't assume any sense is common anymore. Depending on the type of work you are doing, many ethical dilemmas can exist. When anticipating the issues that could arise, think about situations that could occur with customers or clients, as well as internal experiences between employees and you, and employees and each other.

When dealing with the public, your employees may be tempted to withhold information, make unrealistic promises, or sell them things they don't really need. Dealing with the public extends to working with suppliers, where gifts may be used to entice your employees to award business contracts. Instead of hoping they know how to act in these situations, you may want to create a policy, and train employees on what is considered appropriate behavior for the situations they are working in.

Sometimes supervisors are under pressure and ask their employees to do things they might not be comfortable with, for example, changing a few numbers on a report. When the issue involves you, your employees may not feel comfortable coming to you if they think you are being unethical. Assure them that you want them to come to you should this type of situation arise. Take the feedback with an open mind, as discussed earlier, remembering to listen to the message, not the way it is given.

When dealing with each other, whether directly or just by being in the same workplace, your employees may question each other's behaviors. Is it ok to work through coffee break and take a longer lunch? Is it ok to use the photocopier for personal use? Is it ok to eat the food that isn't presentable for customers? You will need to clearly explain what behaviors are allowed, and encourage people to ask if they are unsure. Employees should feel comfortable holding each other accountable to the rules as well. Ethical behavior of all types can be encouraged by having policies, training employees on these policies, enforcing them, and cultivating the corresponding organizational culture.

With respect to unethical behavior, you may have situations where some people believe an action is right, and others believe it's wrong. This is why ethics can be tricky; they stem from individual morals, and these individual morals can be different. One person may feel uncomfortable in a situation that someone else may be fine with. Even though you have done ethical training and set out the rules for acceptable behavior, you may still deal with this type of conflict. Some employees may find that they just can't work in a place where the ethics don't match their own, and you may find there's nothing you can do, or need to do, to fix it for them. They will have to decide if they wish to stay in that environment.

> Have you ever felt uncomfortable with someone's unethical behavior at work? Did you say anything about it? Would it have been appropriate for you to say something? If so, what could you have said? _____
>
> _____
>
> _____

Knowledge sharing. An organization that values learning should also value sharing what people know and how they do things. While knowledge sharing isn't your typical training, building a culture of sharing is important for building human capital. In the world today, more and more of an organization's value comes from what its employees know, how they build relationships, and how they do their service jobs. This is different knowledge to pass along than how to operate a machine. When employees leave our organizations, for whatever reason, this knowledge goes with them. To retain our human capital value, it is important to capture this knowledge.

Employees have two types of knowledge they can share with each other. The first type is very easy to explain, similar to explaining how to operate a machine. When people receive their on-the-job training, it is explicit knowledge that is passed along. Often this information is easy to capture in terms of a step-by-step process or standard operating procedure.

The second type of knowledge is not as easy to explain; it's more about the gift someone has to do what they do very well. It's his finesse in dealing with people, his ability to pick the right course of action each time. This tacit knowledge is not in process format, and you may only be able to capture it if you can capture a person's stories. Asking people about the special ways they build relationships, or the insight they give to certain problems, is also important to be able to do the job well. Encouraging your experienced employees to share this type of knowledge is also very useful; the problem is they may not want to volunteer their secrets. Why would someone share their source of power or success? What's in it for them? If an employee feels secure in his job, he may be willing to share this type of knowledge to make the company better. Having a culture of appreciation is important for encouraging a feeling of security and promoting this type of knowledge sharing between staff members.

> **What type of knowledge do you have about your work that you wouldn't think to readily share with others?** _____
>
> _____
>
> _____
>
> **Would you be willing to share this with others? What would be the benefit to you? To the organization?** _____
>
> _____
>
> _____
>
> _____

Continuous learning. Training can be expensive, and many companies either can't or don't invest in ongoing training. It's important to realize that the company doesn't have to pay for an excessive number of training programs if they just instill a culture of learning, and provide suggestions on how or where people can get more information about their jobs. Employees want to do their jobs better and most would take it upon themselves to learn on their own time. Organizations can build libraries or lists of resources, people included, to point employees in the right direction for their learning.

Talking with employees about their work interests can get them thinking about their careers. An organization can match an employee's career aspirations with available opportunities, and then point out the learning needed to become eligible for the new role. If direction is given, employees will take the initiative to learn on their own. The only reward they need is that they are permitted to use the new skills they have acquired. The supervisor must remain aware of employees' interests and abilities, and allocate work and opportunities accordingly. When the organization is requiring employees to attend training, they should be paid for their time. Reduce the stress on employees by ensuring their regular work duties are covered by someone else while they are away. Again, be sure to offer opportunities for them to use their newly acquired skills, and give them feedback on how they are doing.

Are you learning continuously? What is something you would like to learn for your job right now (other than what you are hoping to learn from this book)? _____

_____

_____

Where would you get this training? _____

_____

Would you be willing to do it on your own if you knew it was important to the organization? _____

Employees value training. Most will say training is a valuable benefit an organization can provide. Taking the time to train someone properly, so he truly understands the task and how to do it safely, is a gift you can give an employee, and is required by law. When an employee is able to do his job well, he will feel good about himself and about the organization. Take this opportunity to build positive relations with your staff.

Being proactive with diversity and ethics training, and modeling the example of being inclusive and supportive, will show employees they are respected and valued. Your efforts early on will prevent conflict and internal struggles later, and lead to more open discussions so people can feel comfortable in their workplaces. In order to fulfill this commitment, it is necessary to adhere to a zero tolerance policy when people break rules.

It may not be enough to have an awareness of other cultures; employees may require help to adapt to working with people from other ethnicities. For example, if an employee is very direct and someone from another culture isn't used to that, he can learn to change the way he comes across to his co-workers. If one culture values relationship-building before working together, you can encourage those types of activities. As you have developed an appreciation for your own culture, you can develop an appreciation for other cultures, and encourage others to do the same. From a *MeYouQ* perspective, a person needs to appreciate him- or herself first before they can appreciate someone else.

Encouraging others to learn and share will not only build human capital, but you will be creating a community of people who help each other and feel comfortable asking questions instead of pretending to know things. They will see each other's strengths and recognize when they need assistance. Not only will this result in fewer mistakes, employees will be able to grow their talents and feel fulfilled in learning and sharing.

Applications for Employee Mental Health

Training activities are important for Psychological Factors 1, 2, 3, 4, 6, 7, 10, 12, and 13.

Psychological Support (PF1) ensures employees can discuss their mental health issues with the manager and be given accommodation where necessary. As a supervisor, you can give psychological support to your new employee during the orientation by:

Offering future assistance. In this early period of relationship building, you can assure the employee that if she ever has issues she needs to talk to you about your door will be open. Let her know that her mental health is important to you, and even if she doesn't have an illness but feels she is becoming stressed, she can come to you.

Would this offer have been useful to you in your work history? What struggles might it have prevented for you? _____

_____

_____

Organizational Culture (PF2) is impacted through training activities that encourage trust and fairness in the organization. As a supervisor, you can see that training activities contribute positively by:

Facilitating knowledge sharing. By appreciating those with experience and ensuring they have a place in the future of your organization, you can encourage them to share their secrets to success. When you have new employees with recent education, conflict may arise because each party thinks they know best. Facilitate the exchange of information and best practices, and get the parties to break down their mental models to consider those of others. Ensure healthy debate as employees work out the best solution to problems. Work on capturing this knowledge for business continuity and reference purposes. Don't forget that people operate under the WIIFM perspective, and there needs to be some sort of remuneration for this information.

Providing training opportunities. All motivated employees should have opportunities to participate in training. Whether someone has performance gaps or is preparing for their next position, all employees, regardless of race, religion, gender, or any other difference, should have an equal opportunity in the workplace. Be sure to have an individual plan for each employee.

Modeling ethical behavior. Employees look to their leaders for cues on how to behave. When you model honesty and respect for others, you will encourage the same type of behavior from your employees. As soon as the supervisor starts to stray from the rules, or permits others to stray, the organization's culture begins to change. For a new employee, those first few days of watching how people work in the organization will set the tone for his performance as well.

Are you comfortable sharing your knowledge? Do you hold back because you want the power of knowing things? What could someone say or do to encourage you to share? _____

_____

_____

Clear Leadership & Expectations (PF3) can be shown during a new employee orientation. This is a good time to define expectations, right at the very beginning of the employee's career with the organization, and before she has a chance to come to different conclusions about what is expected. At this time, you can help the employee see her role by:

Explaining the job fully. Outline the job duties, and set the level of expected performance for the new employee. Ensure she knows what she is supposed to do and how her performance will be measured. Also explain your leadership philosophy and how you will be interacting with her in terms of making decisions and providing other support.

Connecting the job to the organization. Explain to the new employee how her job fits in with the larger organization. Tell her why her role is important, and identify others who depend on her work to do their jobs. Help her understand the potential consequences of underperformance.

If your own boss articulated his or her leadership philosophy and the level of support he or she was prepared to give you, what might he or she say? _____

_____

_____

A Respectful Workplace (PF4) occurs when diversity is valued and appropriate behaviors are encouraged. To encourage respectful behavior and appreciation for internal and external people, you can teach your employees about *MeYouQ*. You can also encourage a positive work atmosphere by:

Encouraging cultural exchanges. Employees may not feel comfortable asking people about their background or the things that make them different. With your employee's permission, you can offer others some insight into who she is, and encourage her co-workers to talk to her about her culture. View differences in a positive light, and don't allow employees to use them to exclude someone from the group. You can do these things regardless of whether you do formal diversity training.

Putting others first. When you put others first and show respect for their needs, you are leading by example. Putting people first means aiding and collaborating; actions that facilitate knowledge sharing. When people want to see each other succeed, they will be more willing to assist them in that endeavor. Encourage employees to care about the success of others.

Holding employees accountable. People may not be respectful by nature. Remember that people have many different backgrounds, and this may or may not have included respectful relationships. Teach people how to treat others with respect and, when they don't, hold them accountable for their behavior and require that they meet the expectations of the workplace.

Understanding knowledge doesn't have to be shared. It would be a mistake to assume that people will share knowledge just because you are expecting them to. Your employees can withhold their best practices and will do so if they don't feel respected and appreciated. Knowledge sharing is doing the company a favor, and you will need to earn their cooperation to get the best results.

What have you done lately to learn about other cultures? List three things you can do to learn more about the people you work with. _____

_____

_____

What have you done lately to learn about your own culture and how you come across to other people? How might your culture's communication practices, work style, or level of formality be different than those of another culture? _____

_____

_____

_____

Growth & Development (PF6) initiatives can reassure employees that they are valued and they have a future in the organization. As a supervisor you can assist in your employees' development by:

Connecting aspirations to opportunities. Once you know what an employee's career aspirations are, you can help him plan for the growth and development activities he will need. When new opportunities come up in the workplace, you can allocate tasks according to this plan.

Remembering the soft skills. It's easy to remember the technical skills required for the job in the development plan, but don't forget about intra- and interpersonal skills; the

MeYouQ skills in recognizing, understanding, and managing all of the things that make each person a unique individual. This will lead to good human relations in the organization.

Encouraging employees. Ask your employees how their developmental activities are going—show an interest. Providing development opportunities may not be enough if your employees believe no one cares whether they develop or not, or they are afraid to try new roles in the organization. Encourage them to try out their new competencies in different situations and allow them to make mistakes while they are learning.

Have you participated in development programs at work? What did the managers do to show an interest in and support you in what you were learning? _____

_____

_____

Recognition & Rewards (PF7) should be used to acknowledge the extra efforts employees contribute towards their learning. Many times, these rewards are intangible and cost the organization nothing. The cost of not using recognition is much greater; employees may become disengaged from their work if they think what they are doing isn't valued. As a supervisor, you can recognize and reward by:

Appreciating efforts. Developmental opportunities help the employee and the organization. When an employee has better

291

soft skills, the work atmosphere will benefit. When an employee has better technical skills, the quality of the work will improve. Be sure to acknowledge the employee's initiative and thank her for the extra work she is taking on.

Providing feedback. To grow and develop, the employee is going to need feedback on how he is performing. When he tries out his new skills with work or with people, be sure to let him know how he did. Your employee will probably not get things completely right the first time, so some corrective feedback will help him learn while he is practicing. A person really cannot develop without feedback.

Acknowledging accomplishments. When an employee has completed a training program, he should be congratulated. When he has gained the ability to do something well after working hard to be able to do it, this should be acknowledged. These types of events are important to a person, and it's going to mean a lot to him if you take the time to recognize his achievement. Bear in mind that some people are uncomfortable with public recognition, so if you plan to make a big announcement about someone's accomplishment, be sure to ask him for permission.

Recognizing team attitudes. Whether it's sharing knowledge or being inclusive with others in the organization, individuals should also be recognized for their efforts. Remember, you don't want to just expect that people will comply with your request that they help others, you need to look at it from the perspective that they are doing a favor for you and the organization. Be sure to appreciate people for their cooperation and for creating a friendly work environment for you and for others.

What has your boss done to recognize your achievements? _____

_____

_____

How did this make you feel? _____

_____

Engagement (PF10) is demonstrated by employees when they expend discretionary effort for the organization. Engagement provides intrinsic value to employees, and they are more likely to become engaged at work when the organization supports them and they feel involved. As supervisor, you can use training to enhance engagement by:

Encouraging continuous improvement. When a person can do her job well, she will get more intrinsic value from doing the work. The more she knows about her job, the better she will function, therefore, providing additional training or resources will help improve performance. When people feel good on the job, they are willing to work harder to feel even better.

Facilitating learning communities. Having positive social groups in the workplace can help people to feel engaged at work. Bringing diverse groups together by adapting to their differences is one way; another way is to encourage employees to learn together. You can bring communities of practice together to learn from each other in their areas of interest and expertise. Introduce your staff to people from other areas of the organization, and provide them with meeting space; for example some organizations have lunch and learn programs, or public speaking groups that decide to meet regularly.

Discussing career plans. Most people want to progress within a company. These days, the hierarchical promotions of the past may not be available or appropriate. It is important to find out what employees are interested in doing and where their strengths lie so they can participate in training, or other opportunities to give them skills for the future, whether it's with your company or another. When people are working towards a goal, they are more likely to be engaged. If you develop someone to a point where he leaves because he doesn't see a future at the company, don't feel like it was a waste. Think of it as a good thing for that person's future and be happy with the contributions he did make. You never know, he may eventually come back when a position does open. Consider that, regardless of the opportunities available, employees may quit if they are not given the chance to grow and develop.

Has anyone discussed your career with you? If they did, what benefits did you realize? If no one did, how might such a discussion have helped you? _____

_____

_____

Psychological Protection (PF12) is facilitated through diversity training and having policies against harassment. As a supervisor you can ensure the protection of your employees' mental health by:

Implementing team rules. Facilitate staff discussions about what is expected from members of the team. Be accommodating for differences only to a point where team performance is not going to suffer. If the team requires members to treat each other a certain way, team rules and/or guidelines should be created. Have them write these down, sign in agreement, and hold each other accountable to them.

Having zero tolerance for harassment. Check your organization's policies on various types of harassment. Ensure your employees know the expectations, and that they can come to you if they feel they are being harassed. If an employee brings information forward about an alleged harasser, be sure to fully investigate the situation. Have zero tolerance for harassment, and investigate every situation, even if you feel the employee might be overreacting. If you find evidence that a policy has been broken, comply with your responsibilities and issue the appropriate consequences. Lean on your human resources department if you have one.

> **Have you sat down with a team to come up with rules before?**
> **List some rules that would help a diverse team to be inclusive**
> **and successful.** _____
> _____
> _____
> _____

Protection of Physical Safety (PF13) is important for employees to feel safe at work and be able to concentrate on their job. As a supervisor, you can show that physical safety is a priority by:

Including safety in your training. When planning your training programs, consider the safety aspect as well. Be aware that people who didn't grow up in your country may need extra safety training—even safety training in their preferred language—to ensure they completely understand. In some cultures employees would never question the boss, so encourage all employees to address their safety concerns with you.

> **Which aspects of safety should be covered when someone is new**
> **to your organization?** _____
> _____
> _____
> _____

Chapter 26 Takeaways:

↗ Use the job instruction method for effective employee training; don't skip any steps

↗ Provide a comprehensive orientation so new employees feel they fit in and are supported

↗ Use diversity training for awareness of differences and appropriate behavior

↗ Include ethics training to ensure everyone knows the expected behavior when working with people within and outside of your organization

↗ Build a culture of learning and knowledge sharing to grow and retain human capital

↗ Encourage informal learning; let employees know you value that they take the initiative to learn on their own

↗ Ensure employees feel they can come to you with training and safety questions, harassment and ethical issues, and for career

↗ Applications for Psychological Health and
Safety include: offering future assistance,
facilitating knowledge sharing, providing
training opportunities, modeling ethical
behavior, explaining the job fully, connecting
the job to the organization, encouraging
cultural exchanges, putting others first,
holding employees accountable,
understanding knowledge doesn't have to be
shared, connecting aspirations to
opportunities, remembering the soft skills,
encouraging employees, appreciating efforts,
acknowledging accomplishments, recognizing
team attitudes, encouraging continuous
improvement, facilitating learning
communities, discussing career plans,
implementing team rules, having zero
tolerance for harassment, and including safety
in your training

The expectations used in your training and performance
management programs must be consistent to give your
employees every opportunity to be capable and succeed in your
organization. A performance management program will assist in
keeping employees on track.

Chapter 27: Performance Management

Do you know the importance of giving feedback to employees?

A PERFORMANCE MANAGEMENT PROGRAM is needed to help attain organizational goals. A performance appraisal may be an annual thing, but performance management is ongoing. The supervisor needs to ensure employees' goals align with the larger organizational goals, and set the expectations for performance. He or she then provides suitable training to ensure employees have the skills required to perform their jobs and manages their performance by giving them feedback.

The annual appraisal. When performance is only discussed once a year, it's not receiving enough attention. While you might provide a formal, written performance appraisal once a year to determine pay increases or goals for the next year, discussions and feedback about performance should be more regular. You shouldn't be waiting a year to discuss something that can be improved now, just as you shouldn't wait a year to recognize an employee for excellent work. Evidence to support the annual review should also be collected regularly, to avoid basing a rating strictly on information gathered just before the appraisal.

Be objective. Your HR department will provide employee rating forms, but if you are a small organization, you may have to develop your own. Be sure to only include factors relevant to the work the employee is doing, and to rate on factors that are under their control. The most important part of the appraisal is your ability to observe and rate your employees objectively. Base the rating on performance, not on your personal opinion of the employee. Be fair with your ratings and comments, ensuring that you can substantiate them with concrete examples. If you are using a scale, be sure to define each rating so you have clear criteria for evaluating performance in order to arrive at a score; for example, specify what an employee has to do to earn a 5 out of 5.

Two-way conversation. Employees are more likely to accept the performance appraisal process if they are given a voice. Allow employees to ask questions about, and even to challenge, their ratings. Some organizations allow the employee to self-assess, and then the employee and supervisor sit down to compare their ratings and discuss discrepancies. The performance appraisal meeting should be a partnership in that way. The two parties should sit down together and discuss the evaluation, instead of the supervisor being the only one who gets to give an opinion.

Focus on the positive. During the performance appraisal meeting, keep things positive and forward-looking. Some supervisors believe in sandwich feedback; you say something positive, give the negative comment, and follow up with another positive. Some people believe the negative message gets lost in the positive with this method, so that's something to consider as well. If you have something negative to say, say it once and let it go. If the employee has heard and acknowledged you, don't belabor the point; focusing on the topic any longer than necessary will only have a negative impact on the relationship.

Create a follow-up plan. At the end of a performance discussion, new goals or a plan for action should be set, along with a timeline for follow-up. Training might be the answer to a performance gap, and specific plans should be made. If an employee is performing well, appreciation or a reward should be given. Good employees should be involved in development plans for future opportunities. Alternatively, an employee may have excellent performance but a poor attitude, which results in a different discussion and perhaps a warning that the attitude needs to improve.

Have you had a performance appraisal done? What did the supervisor do in that meeting that was really good? _____

_____

_____

What did the supervisor do that you would want to do differently? _____

_____

The appraisal and daily activities involved in managing performance have the potential for relationship-breaking. It is so important to carefully choose how to give necessary feedback, and for the employee to believe that you are sincerely trying to help her. Consider diversity in your employees and how you might have to change your message for the particular audience.

"You" language should be avoided if it implies you are blaming the employee, as when a person becomes defensive, he is not going to receive the message you are trying to convey. Also, stick to objective, observable examples of behavior and don't attack the employee's personality. Use caring words so people don't get emotional and to show support for the employee. Reassure him that you can make a plan for him to improve, and that he is having typical struggles that many people share.

Finally, do your best to ensure the employee feels better leaving the meeting than she did coming in. A performance appraisal meeting shouldn't be feared, it should be a productive discussion. The employee should feel supported and be forward-looking with goals for the future.

Applications for Employee Mental Health

Positive performance management is important for Psychological Factors 4, 8, and 9.

Civility & Respect (PF4) is about being respectful and considerate during interactions with each other. As a supervisor, you can enhance the performance discussion by:

Filtering messages. Your employee may not be a perfect communicator. The way he states his point of view, or questions you during the performance discussion, may seem as if he is attacking you or being argumentative. It's important to be able to filter out what he is trying to say and respond to that, instead of responding to his tone of voice or words he might be using inappropriately.

Maintaining confidence. If you have done a good job of observing and rating the employee, you should not fear delivering the message. When you choose appropriate, respectful wording to convey your message, you should be successful. Be confident that you can handle any conflict that comes up during the meeting, and focus on maintaining the relationship.

Anticipating disagreement. It's likely that the employee will have some questions, or will differ in his opinion of his performance, or the reasons for poor performance. Be respectful and dedicate yourself to having the problem-solving discussion. You won't always agree with other people, but you can agree to have the type of conversation required to figure out a solution. Consider that you may need to step back from your position to reach a workable compromise.

Give an example of a situation where you had to give someone feedback on his or her performance and you didn't think it would be well-received. _____

_____

_____

How did you deliver the feedback and what should you have done differently? _____

_____

_____

Involvement & Influence (PF8) can be part of your performance management discussions. Employees may want to have a say in how their work is done and assessed. You can allow employees this type of involvement in their job by:

Asking for their ideas. You might like things done a certain way and train employees to use a certain method, but it's important to realize there is usually more than one way to do something. The people doing the job may have great suggestions on time or cost savings measures, so ask for their ideas. Some companies provide rewards when an employee's idea saves the company money, even though employees might be happy just to benefit from a better way of doing their job.

Encouraging ongoing discussions. Be open to employees' ideas about their jobs. Give the idea honest consideration before saying, "No." If you disagree with the idea, or don't believe it will work, communicate that clearly to the employee. Encourage the person to rethink things and come back with a new plan.

> **Instead of saying, "No" the next time someone makes a suggestion to you, what are you going to say?** _____
>
> _____
>
> _____

Workload Management (PF9) could be an issue that comes up in a performance management discussion. If an employee is struggling in his duties or having performance gaps, the reason might be that he is overloaded. You can be fair to the employee by:

Exploring all possible causes. It would be unrealistic to think that poor performance is always the employee's fault. Organizational processes, systems, and rules could be to blame, or perhaps the job is dependent on someone else's work that isn't getting done. Before jumping to conclusions that a person needs retraining, or isn't getting a pay increase, be sure the cause of poor performance is not something outside of the employee's control.

Having realistic expectations. It can be dangerous to compare employees to each other and expect their abilities to be equal. Just because one of your employees is really good at a certain aspect of her job, it doesn't mean that other employees will measure up just as well. Before discussing your expectations with an employee, be sure to have a very good idea of her ability and potential. Setting overly high expectations could be very frustrating, and cause her to become discouraged or give up.

Give an example of a performance problem you have seen that was caused by something other than the employee's lack of ability. _____

_____

_____

Chapter 27 Takeaways:

↗ Manage employee performance through a system of setting standards, providing ongoing feedback, assessing performance together with the employee, and creating a follow-up plan with training, development, and/or rewards

↗ Be objective by rating only factors under the employee's control and using a standardized rating scale

↗ Focus on being positive and forward-looking when discussing the performance appraisal results

↗ Applications for Psychological Health and Safety include: filtering messages, maintaining confidence, anticipating disagreement, asking for their ideas, encouraging ongoing discussions, exploring all possible causes, and having realistic expectations

The way you handle a performance appraisal can affect an employee's motivation. Various motivation theories can be applied in your everyday interactions with employees.

Chapter 28: Employee Motivation

What effect can you have on employee motivation?

SOME MOTIVATION THEORIES DISCUSS inner drives people have. Maslow's hierarchy of needs ranges from the need for safety, food, and shelter on the lower end, to the need to be accepted by others or feel good about oneself on the higher end. While he thought that lower level needs needed to be satisfied before higher level ones, other theorists have said a person can go back and forth between lower and higher level needs at different times, but one need is usually more pressing at a given time than the others. An employee with a lower level need may be worried she can't pay the bills this month, or she won't have a job next month. This person could be motivated with a raise or reassurance that her job is secure. An employee with a higher level need may want to have a challenge in his work, or have successes that make him feel good about himself. This employee could be motivated by development or being put in charge of a team project.

Vroom's expectancy theory is a different type of motivation theory that doesn't focus as much on the types of needs that people have, but more on their ability to cognitively select a specific behavior due to what they believe the end result will be; they weigh the options. Expectancy theory maintains that people will be motivated to choose one behavior over another based on the desirability of the outcome; the reward being offered is something they value, they believe they can achieve the task, and they are confident the reward will be given. To implement this theory, it's important to know what your employee values, ensure she has the support and resources required to be successful, and provide the reward to her when the task is complete. If the employee faces barriers in completing the task, or if she wasn't given a deserved reward in the past, she is not going to be motivated.

Herzberg's two-factor theory of motivation states that certain factors in the workplace provide job satisfaction and do indeed motivate people. These are things like giving workers responsibility and appreciation, and having good employee relations. Other workplace factors, such as pay, benefits, vacation, and job security, only serve to prevent dissatisfaction. While it is important to prevent dissatisfaction in the workplace, it is also important to motivate your employees; you need to do a combination of both.

McLelland's acquired needs theory states that individuals have the highest need in one of three areas: achievement, power, or affiliation. If you know which of these needs is highest for your employee, you can assign work and create an environment that will be motivating for them. An employee with a need for achievement likes to be challenged and reach goals as a result of her own efforts; assigning her a project or giving her problem solving tasks would be motivating. An employee with a need for power will place a high value on being in charge and making decisions that will further his status and recognition; assigning him to lead a team would be motivating. An employee with a need for affiliation enjoys social relationships, she will prefer working in teams, or having a collaborative workplace; assigning her to be part of the social committee, or to provide service to others would be motivating.

Knowing what motivates your employees is important because you want to provide the correct incentive for them and be able to drive their behavior. Offering money and bonuses are tangible items, whereas recognition and appreciation are intangibles. Both of these are extrinsic types of rewards because the employee relies on someone else to provide them. Some individuals have an internal drive and are motivated intrinsically by their successes. It's important not to rely exclusively on an employee's intrinsic motivation; you must provide a variety of extrinsic rewards too. However, by hiring people with a propensity for intrinsic motivation, those who get personal satisfaction out of their work, you will find you have to motivate less.

The theories all have something to offer with respect to discovering what drives employees. Different employees will have different needs, and different things motivate different people. Offering a trip for two to Hawaii as a prize may be meaningless to a single parent with three kids, who couldn't use the vacation anyway. Offering money to someone when she will just have to pay half of it in tax is not likely to be very motivating either. Giving someone extra time off won't be motivating if he has nothing to do at home and prefers to be at work. Get to know your individual employees and what works for each of them. Also consider that some of the more intangible rewards may be motivating to many of your employees; you can't go wrong with showing you value people, and developing them for future opportunities.

What are three needs you are trying to fill? _____

_____

_____

What tangible and intangible things could your workplace offer to motivate you? _____

_____

_____

 Think about your own motivators, they are not likely to be the same as what motivates others, and they can change at any time. As you focus on your relationships with others, and encourage your employees to be open with you, you can have discussions that will allow you to figure out what their individual needs are, and what would be motivating to them. By talking to them about their personal motivators, you are treating them individually and showing them they are important. Be prepared to follow through with action after these discussions with employees, as you will lose trust if you pretend to care and then do nothing about it.

Applications for Employee Mental Health

Motivating employees is important for Psychological Factors 5, 7, and 8.

Psychological Competencies & Requirements (PF5) can be achieved as you have discussions with your employees about their needs and their comfort level with different tasks. Once you know what would motivate them and what they are capable of, you can help your employees by:

Assigning appropriate work. Placing an employee in a role that suits his natural drivers and interpersonal abilities will set him up for success. He will feel competent and interested in the work he is doing, and be more engaged and comfortable in his job. When you get to know your employees better, you can match them to the right positions in the organization. If it turns out that an employee is in the wrong job, you can work to place him more appropriately.

Preparing employees. Your discussions may uncover things that employees would like to achieve, but they may not have the skills to be successful at. Get them the proper training before you move them into a new role, so they are able to excel. If the job is going to be outside of the scope of their ability, even after training, find a different role for them where they can have their needs met. The idea is to set employees up for success by putting them in the right positions and giving them the tools they need to succeed. Helping them to understand themselves through *MeYouQ*, and getting them to see how they can relate better to others, will prepare them with interpersonal skills for their position.

> **What kind of development could you give an introverted employee who wants to make more money by working in a sales position?** _____
>
> _____
>
> _____

Recognition & Reward (PF7) is about not taking employees for granted. Your discussions about what motivates your staff will help you to implement a recognition and reward program that is valued. Once you decide to use motivation theories in a serious way, you can increase your impact by:

Remembering to reward. A supervisor's life is busy. It's easy to get distracted by production demands and other issues that come up each day. Weeks can go by very quickly, so you need to keep track of who you should be appreciating and rewarding. It may sound silly, but if you don't keep a list of names and what you have promised, or when you should follow up with people, you're going to forget.

Rewarding with something valued. A five-year pin may not be an exciting reward for people in today's workforce. Employees might not be able to keep up their intrinsic motivation if an extrinsic one takes too long to arrive. Some organizations like to reward with an object the employee will have for a long time, instead of just cash. Gift cards are a good option as well, because the person will be more likely to choose something special. A fun assignment, or a choice of work duties can also be a great reward; the important thing is to know what will be motivating to your specific, individual employees.

Using tangible and intangible rewards. Organizations may have limited resources for fancy rewards programs. While it's nice to occasionally receive something tangible, intangible rewards can easily be given and in many cases are just as valuable. The idea is to give your appreciation and recognition in a sincere way and when it is actually earned. If you give appreciation for every little thing the employee is supposed to be doing as part of her job, the praise might get lost when something larger occurs. If someone is already intrinsically motivated, you may be removing that motivation if you offer an extrinsic reward once and then not again; the intrinsic motivation may not return. A mix of rewards is great, and following a well-thought out plan is important.

What is one tangible reward in your workplace? _____

_____

How might this motivate one person but not another? _____

_____

_____

Think about a certain individual in your department. What is one intangible reward he or she would appreciate? _____

_____

Involvement & Influence (PF8) is about giving employees some say in different aspects of their jobs; this can include what motivates them. As a supervisor, you can ensure employees have a say by:

Having ongoing discussions. As employee needs change from time to time, it's important to have ongoing discussions about new needs they might be seeking to fulfill. The idea behind some motivation theories is that once a need is satisfied, employees will seek to fill a different one. Just when you think you know what employees want, it could all change! Encourage employees to discuss their work interests and desired rewards with you as they evolve, while recognizing that you can only do your best to meet their needs and may not be able to implement changes immediately.

What can you do if someone expresses their desires to you, but you don't see an immediate opportunity to satisfy their needs?

_____

_____

_____

Give an example of a time when you had a need met at work and, following that event, a very different need popped up. _____

_____

_____

_____

Chapter 28 Takeaways:

↗ Use the principles behind motivation theories to be more in touch with an employee's individual needs, or the rewards he or she seeks

↗ Consider that real motivators might be those things that make employees feel good about themselves and their work, like responsibility and appreciation

↗ Recognize that some individuals are naturally inclined to be motivated, but they should still be rewarded at times

↗ Applications for Psychological Health and Safety include: assigning appropriate work, preparing employees, remembering to reward, rewarding with something valued, using tangible and intangible rewards, and have ongoing discussions

Motivation can decrease drastically when information is not being shared and rumors start. When the organization is going through a major change, a well thought out process is required. This will lessen the negative impact on morale and productivity.

Chapter 29: Change Management

Have you noticed that many people don't like change?

CHANGE IS CONSTANT IN THE WORLD today, and your organization is likely not exempt. Change can be a big cause of stress for employees because it involves a certain level of discomfort. Employees may resist change because they don't see the need for it, they may gossip about what they think is going on, or they may be comfortable with the way things are and be disinclined to expend the extra effort involved in moving to a new way of doing things. When employees are not involved in decision making, they may be subject ofo a new initiative they know nothing about, without having had a say in how it's implemented. When the benefits of the change are not communicated to them, they won't understand why the change is important. When details about the change are not given to them, they will worry about what it means for them, and start inventing their own stories about what they think is going to happen. This resistance to change can affect your organization's ability to quickly and successfully implement important changes.

For all of these reasons, when implementing change, you will need a good change management process. Change shouldn't be made unless it is necessary or beneficial. Before planning the change, you need to understand its potential impact on your people. When rolling out the change, you are going to need support from employees, and after the change is implemented you want to ensure all of your systems are updated to reflect the new way of doing things. A good change management process involves preparation, communication, and a plan for implementation.

Conduct fact finding. When looking at a new system or process for your organization, it's important to understand the functionality of the existing one. Determine how your employees are using the current system to do their work, and whether they have any customization that helps them do their job more efficiently, for example, templates they use to generate reports. The new system may need to include these features so work is not disrupted. Also, ask employees what is lacking in the current system that would help them to do their jobs better. When making a change for one reason, you might be able to solve problems in other areas at the same time. Doing this will create real benefit and help you gain support for the change from employees.

Get employees onboard early. Not everyone is going to be excited, or even willing to change. Some of your employees may like change and be more receptive to continuous improvement ideas. These are the employees you want to initially involve in the change, so they can act as your champions; it is important to have supporters who are able to influence the other employees.

Communicate details. Before too many rumors begin to circulate, it's important to announce the change to your department. Be sure to give a consistent message, so all employees get the same information, and deliver it to all employees equally. If you don't have much information to share at first, let them know that. Ask them to trust that you will provide more information as soon as you can, and that you will provide it equally to everyone. Provide details in multiple formats; for example, if you have a meeting to make an announcement, follow it up with a written record of what you said.

Use phased implementation. When dealing with a major change, you can avoid having multiple problems at once by breaking the project into phases. This will allow you to work out the problems in one area before having to worry about another area. This approach may provide insight into issues you hadn't thought of, and allow you to do more planning before moving on.

Allow for a learning curve. Employees will need to be trained in the new way of doing things and new support materials may need to be created. Initially, as they begin to use the new methods, they are not going to be as productive as they were with the old system. Employees should not be at a pay disadvantage during this time, and they should also be allowed to learn from their mistakes. Do not place undue pressure on people while they are learning a new system, or they will surely decide they do not like the change.

Show appreciation. Change takes extra effort, and employees should feel that you appreciate them in this undertaking. Be positive about the change, and encourage them to be positive as well. Recognize their contributions during this time. Your positive comments on their behavior will reinforce their efforts, and motivate them to continue working toward the final outcome.

Update related systems. New ways of doing things are going to mean new goals and new performance appraisals, possibly new reward systems, or adjustments to workloads or job descriptions. To ensure barriers to performance are not created, the change must flow through all affected departments concurrently. This will solidify the change and prevent old methods from creeping back into use.

Recall a time when a change was implemented poorly in your organization. What were the big mistakes they made?

_____

_____

_____

Your compassion for people in a change process is important for its successful implementation. Remember, people are individuals and will respond uniquely. Recognize the stress and confusion that can be caused, and talk things through with employees. Help them to manage their emotions, and be realistic about what is happening and why. Listen to their concerns, and help them to feel validated. Acknowledge their struggles and their points of view, and be forthcoming with details about the change.

A period of change can also put extra stress on you. Continue to practice good human relations while your stress level is rising. Don't hesitate to ask your employees for time to think before responding to requests if you need it. Stay aware of the pressures on you and manage your behavior. Become aware and remain aware.

Applications for Employee Mental Health

Good change management is important for Psychological Factors 2, 3, 7, 8, and 9.

Organizational Culture (PF2) is based partly on having trust in the workplace. Having secrets about a change, or not communicating properly about it, can cause employees to become distrustful. You can enhance the feeling of trust during a change by:

Communicating early. Don't give the rumor mill time to start before you let employees know that something is going on. You don't need to have all the information before providing them with some of the details.

Considering the impact. Consider who the change is going to impact and how. The best way to do this is to begin to talk to people about the idea and get their thoughts. Have some meetings, or call together some focus groups of people who can share this feedback with you. Ask informal leaders to participate, as they are likely to have insight into how people feel.

What happens at your workplace when people aren't given enough information about what's going on? _____

_____

_____

Clear Leadership & Expectations (PF3) is important during a time of change. As a supervisor, you should be:

Communicating the vision. Be clear about the direction of the change when you make the big announcement to everyone. Think ahead of time about the questions employees will have, and be prepared with clear and direct answers. If you are unsure about something, don't pretend to be sure. If you can't offer good reasons for the change, or what the change entails, people will not be inclined to support you.

Carrying people through. Employees are going to experience struggles with a new system and will want to return to the way they were doing things before. Be prepared for these moments; remind employees why the change is needed and how you can help them during the transition. Continue to communicate the vision.

Setting new standards. Changes in work likely mean expectations have changed as well. You may have to meet with each employee to discuss the impact on his job and performance standards.

Have you struggled with a change before? What kinds of emotions can you expect from employees going through this type of experience? _____

_____

_____

Recognition & Reward (PF7) should be considered during a time of change. As a supervisor, it is important to realize the discomfort change can bring, and assist your employees by:

Acknowledging extra effort. Don't expect people to put in extra effort out of their dedication to the organization. Recognize that employees are going over and above their regular duties in support of you and the organization. Think positively about how they are helping, even if they are complaining.

Expressing appreciation. When employees accept the change and support you, a thank you should be given. Let them know their cooperation was important to you, and that implementation of the change was successful due to their efforts. Let them know you appreciate their teamwork and their positive attitudes.

Do employees at your workplace complain when they have to do extra things? How can you change the way they look at these situations? _____

_____

_____

Involvement & Influence (PF8) is important when making a major change in an organization. Gaining employee buy-in and cooperation can be achieved by:

Involving employees in planning. If employees have had the opportunity to offer input during the planning phase, they are more likely to go along with the change, even if it isn't exactly what they wanted. When employees are part of the planning discussions, they become aware of the reasons certain actions are being taken while others are not.

Asking employees for their perspectives. Allowing employees to be involved early on will give you an opportunity to see how the change might impact them. You may not have thought of everything in your planning, so it's important to gain this useful information to avoid issues later.

Adapting to employee needs. Gaining the employees' perspective allows you to integrate this information into your planning efforts. If a small change now will mean avoiding a problem later, then it's worth it to take the time now. If an employee request doesn't seem reasonable, some critical thinking may uncover an option not previously considered.

What are the pros and cons of involving employees in decisions?

_____

_____

_____

How can you do things differently to convert the cons into pros?

_____

_____

_____

_____

Workload Management (PF9) may become an issue during change because of the extra time needed for learning and transitioning. At this time it may be difficult for employees to handle their regular work and implement the required change. The supervisor can reduce stressors by:

Getting assistance. Recognize the time commitment involved in the change, and consider this extra demand on employees. Work to get them additional help with their tasks, or reduce the regular workload temporarily.

Reducing pressure. While deadlines can be motivating, unreasonable ones can cause too much pressure on an employee. Talk with your employees about the demands on their time and make adjustments to deadlines where possible, without affecting the overall project's critical path. Also, consider that after a period of extra work, employees may need a break. Keep track of the extra efforts, and ensure people aren't being overworked. Extra compensation may be required, especially if you are expecting employees to work overtime.

How can you approach management to delay a deadline because employees are overworked? What would you say? _____

_____

_____

_____

_____

Chapter 29 Takeaways:

↗ Help to relieve employee stress during change by helping them to see why it's necessary

↗ Use good change management practices that include: gathering information about employee needs, using change champions, sharing information early, introducing the change in phases, being patient and thankful, and sticking with it until everyone has converted to the new method

↗ Applications for Psychological Health and Safety include: communicating early, considering the impact, communicating the vision, carrying people through, setting new standards, acknowledging extra effort, expressing appreciation, involving employees in planning, asking employees for their perspectives, adapting to employee needs, getting assistance, and reducing pressure

Some people will not support change, or may not adhere to organizational rules and policies. When employees are not meeting expectations, you may need to have difficult conversations with them.

Chapter 30: Difficult Conversations

Are you able to maintain relationships when reprimanding employees?

AS MUCH AS YOU TRY TO BUILD relations and help others build their *MeYouQ*, you will have difficult situations to deal with from time to time. Situations such as a change in behavior, or the breaking of a rule, will require a special type of conversation. For these difficult conversations, you can follow this strategy:

1. **Have a private conversation.** Ask to speak to the employee in private, but don't give her too much time to worry about the meeting; perhaps a ten-minute warning is enough.
2. **Ensure the timing is right.** If the employee is busy meeting a deadline at work, don't disrupt that for a meeting. If you are upset about the situation, allow yourself time to calm down before having the conversation.
3. **Build rapport.** When the employee comes into your office, thank her for coming, ask her how her day is going, and be friendly.
4. **Be direct.** Don't ask her, "Do you know why I called you in here today?" Just let her know that you have noticed

there is an issue. Say, "The reason I called you in here today is…"

5. **Ask for an explanation.** Before trying to guess why she is doing what she is doing, or telling her what she needs to do to solve the problem, ask for her side of the story. You may find the response is something you could not have anticipated.

6. **Listen.** Focus on your employee. Look for nonverbal language that may add to the message she is giving you. Don't allow yourself to get distracted by trying to think of a response, focus on listening at this time.

7. **Acknowledge.** Before giving your side of the story or explaining what improvement you need to see, let the person know you hear her, and you can see why she did what she did, or thinks the way she thinks.

8. **State what you need.** You have decided to have this conversation, so it's clear you need the behavior to stop. Tell her what affect her behavior can have on the organization, and let her know that it can't continue.

9. **Problem-solve.** Ask the employee how she is going to solve the problem. Talk it out with her until you come up with something you can both agree to.

10. **Commit to action.** Restate what you have agreed on, and explain what the follow-up will be—who will do what by when.

11. **Follow up.** Keep track of your action plan, fulfill your side of the arrangement, and have a follow-up meeting when you said you would. Upon follow-up, you may find that a new conversation is required, possibly a disciplinary one.

Now that you have an approach to use for difficult conversations, have a look at these typical workplace situations that require intervention from the supervisor: where behavior has changed, where an addiction is determined, and where a rule has been broken.

Behavior has changed. A normally good employee may experience periodic declines in performance. While you probably don't want to make a big deal out of every little issue, and you might even ignore something the first time with the hope it won't happen again, a change in behavior might require an exploratory conversation. The problem isn't necessarily that a rule has been broken; it could be something like a slowdown of performance or a change in attitude. Left unchecked, this behavior could lead to something worse, or could set a bad example for other employees to follow. It could also affect the morale of the people who work with this person, so it's important to address a behavior that appears to be habit-forming.

Your strategy for an exploratory conversation is to follow the steps above, while ensuring the employee feels supported. You may uncover personal issues that you are not qualified to give advice on. If your organization has an Employee and Family Assistance Plan (EFAP), you could refer the employee for counseling. Either way, the situation may require accommodation on your part. Can you adjust a person's schedule so he can take care of family issues? Can you give him an alternate work assignment to relieve him of a negative situation? Have the kind of conversation necessary to figure out the best solution to the problem, and be very clear about what you are prepared to do and what you expect in return. Follow up in writing.

Addiction is determined. In some jurisdictions you will be required to help someone with an addiction to drugs or alcohol to get the help he or she needs. Different rules may apply, but it could mean that if a person wants to keep her job, she has to admit she has a problem and she wants help. You are going to have to engage in a difficult conversation to problem solve this issue. Once again, use your EFAP for the rehabilitation services the employee will need, and reassure her she will have a job when she returns. If the person doesn't agree to get help, the issue would become one of discipline. If an employee is under the influence at work and does something wrong, you might jump from a verbal warning to a suspension. You may need to take someone off the job immediately; however it's always best to seek legal advice, if possible, before making a costly decision.

Rule has been broken. Use of your organization's progressive discipline process will be required in cases where an employee is breaking the rules; such as being late for work, failing to call in when taking a sick day, or not fulfilling her duties. Typically, progressive discipline starts with a verbal warning, followed by a written warning, suspension, and finally, termination. Each step in the discipline process must be documented to build a case for *just cause* dismissal. Each time the employee is warned, she must be told what penalty will follow if the behavior doesn't stop and, if appropriate, what the organization is going to do to help her improve her performance. Also, you shouldn't consolidate unrelated offences in the same case of discipline; if someone is getting a second warning, it should be related to the first offence.

Some rules are too important to use progressive discipline, and result in a stiffer penalty or an instant just cause dismissal. If someone is violent, steals, or is guilty of insubordination, there is just cause for dismissal, usually no notice or pay in lieu of notice is required. When these situations occur, seek help from your human resources department and the management team. Where a union or employee committee is in place, there may be special procedures to follow for disciplinary action or a dismissal.

Suppose you had to talk to Allen because he called in sick, but someone reported seeing him at a different job. Go through the 11 steps of Difficult Conversations and write down what you would say or do.

1. Have a private conversation. _____

_____

2. Ensure the timing is right. _____

_____

3. Build rapport. _____

_____

4. Be direct. _____

_____

5. Ask for an explanation. _____

_____

6. Listen. _____

_____

7. Acknowledge. _____

_____

8. State what you need. _____

_____

9. Problem solve. _____

_____

---

10. Commit to action. _____

_____

11. Follow up. _____

_____

 You're going to have to deal with tough issues and have difficult conversations with some employees. Go into these uncomfortable conversations with the attitude that you want to solve the problem, and help the employee become productive again. Believe that most people will appreciate the second chance, and will work hard to improve. Keep an open mind during the conversation, and recognize your employee's story is coming from his individual experiences and perspective—the way he sees the world. Manage your emotions and his as well, while focusing on the issue and facts. Use your strategies in active listening and "I" language. Agree on as much as possible, but recognize that compromise may be required. Remember you might not share the same view of reality, so you may need to deal with his perceptions.

Applications for Employee Mental Health

Being able to handle a difficult conversation is important for Psychological Factors 1, 2, 4, 11 and 13.

Psychological Support (PF1) can be provided to employees through a difficult conversation. You can provide needed support to your employees by:

Broaching the subject. An employee may be nervous about discussing a mental illness that has been causing him to be problematic at work. He might be worried about being stigmatized, or may think he can handle the situation on his own. If you initiate the conversation you can ensure the employee gets the support he needs.

Do you tend to shy away from difficult conversations because you don't want the conflict? What would you say to encourage yourself to have an uncomfortable conversation with one of your employees? _____

_____

_____

Positive Organizational Culture (PF2) occurs when there is fairness in the workplace. If certain employees are breaking the rules, other employees will be upset, and morale and productivity will suffer. You can help to promote fairness in the workplace by:

Dealing with issues early. Once you develop the confidence to have difficult conversations, you will be able to protect the culture in your organization by having these types of discussions when they become necessary. You can determine what is going on, work on solutions, and hold people accountable. This will increase trust in the workplace.

Being honest with employees. Your ability to get things out in the open by engaging in a difficult conversation allows you to be honest with employees and get honesty from them in return. Honesty will also lead to trust in the workplace.

Why do you think employees are not honest with their bosses all the time? _____

_____

_____

What will you do to increase the chance of employees being honest with you in these difficult situations? _____

_____

_____

Civility & Respect (PF4) includes the interactions between a supervisor and their employees. You can have respectful conversations if you use the difficult conversations strategy properly, which includes:

Using respectful words. Blaming employees or attacking their personalities is not a respectful way to solve a problem. When you follow the steps of listening and acknowledging, and then work on a solution together, employees will feel respected. Use supportive statements such as, "I know we can resolve this issue together," and, "I value your contributions and want to help you succeed."

> **Write down two more supportive statements you can use in a difficult conversation.** _____
>
> _____
>
> _____
>
> _____
>
> _____

Balance (PF11) between work and personal life may be difficult for some employees. You never know what issue someone is facing at home and whether they are able to cope with it. You can help an employee with work-life balance by:

Encouraging honesty. Make it safe for the employee to confide in you about what is causing the disruption at work. Assure her you won't judge, you just want to help. Be prepared for anything and keep your body language in check so she doesn't feel embarrassed. Listen to her whole story and help her work through it, being careful not to overstep professional boundaries and offering only the advice or assistance you are qualified to give. If you have a human resources department, you might send her there for accommodation instead.

Protection of Physical Safety (PF13) may be an added benefit resulting from a difficult conversation. You can help an employee avoid potential future incidents by:

Removing distractions. Intervene before a situation gets out of control, and have the type of conversation that is necessary to change the behavior. Have confidence in the fact that you are intervening to help protect the employee. Your early action can help a person avoid time off work by preventing an injury.

Implementing discipline. Safety legislation means the employer is responsible for safety training and supervision. You need to prepare employees to do their jobs safely, provide proper protective equipment, ensure they use it, and make sure they are following the safety procedures. When employees are noncompliant, you must take serious action; failure to do so is negligent. You can use the difficult conversation strategy to address these issues as well.

What kinds of safety risks could arise in your organization if workers became distracted? _____

_____

_____

What steps does your organization take to prevent these situations from occurring? _____

_____

_____

Chapter 30 Takeaways:

↗ Approach difficult conversations in private and at the right time

↗ Build rapport, but get right to the point. Avoid guessing games

↗ Listen to the employee's explanation; acknowledge her truth

↗ Set expectations, solve problems, gain commitment, and plan to follow up

↗ Applications for Psychological Health and Safety include: broaching the subject, dealing with issues early, being truthful with employees, using respectful words, encouraging honesty, removing distractions, and implementing discipline

Difficult conversations was the last bit of theory. Move on now to mentally prepare for the road ahead. Keep in mind that you can contact the author through the meyouqbook.com website to purchase customized training or coaching to further enhance your skills.

Wrapping Up: Get Ready to be a Great Supervisor

Are you ready for this new chapter in your life?

YOU ARE READY TO LOOK AFTER YOUR employees' mental health, but don't forget to look after your own mental health as well. Choose the right attitude and actions for your position. Your inner voice may work against you on occasion, telling you you're not capable, or causing you to second-guess yourself. Recognize when this is happening, and tell yourself a different story. Your inner voice may also say negative things about your employees, like they are incompetent or uncaring. When that voice speaks up you will need to recognize its destructive power and fight against it. Become aware and remain aware.

Other predictable situations that may arise include: withdrawing when things get tough, not knowing how to do certain aspects of the job, being accused of micromanaging your employees, getting annoyed with the people you work with, and losing your sense of self in your effort to be a people-pleaser. Solutions for these types of problems will be discussed now.

Accepting the challenge. When your inner voice tells you the job is too difficult and it would be best to quit, or when things actually do get rough and you feel like quitting, you can take the view that you are right where you are supposed to be. Think of it in a spiritual way: you are supposed to be learning the lesson being presented to you. You are going through this experience to learn something you will need to know to help you deal with a future event. Even if you aren't a spiritual person, taking this view can be a good coping mechanism.

This isn't to say that you should never change your mind about a decision you have made; humans don't always make the right choices. But recognize that your mind can play games and work against you—be mindful about what is happening and add logic to the feelings you are having.

Ask for help. You probably don't know what you don't know. If employees are complaining about you, it could be for good reason. Listen to their complaints, look objectively at yourself and your performance, and determine whether their comments are warranted. Don't be afraid to admit that you don't know something. Information is available everywhere these days, and your colleagues will have considerable knowledge, too. Reach out to other managers for mentoring and answers to your questions. Read books, watch videos, and take courses. While you expect an attitude of continuous improvement from your employees, expect it from yourself as well.

Manage, don't micromanage. A great way to have conflict with employees is to not trust them to do their jobs. Bosses that micromanage their employees are constantly checking up on them and directing their efforts. If you set proper expectations and train employees well, you should be able to trust them to do

339

their jobs. Resist the temptation to jump in and do their jobs for them, or to be hovering over them while they are working. Remember there are multiple ways to do the same thing; each person will have his own way of doing the job, and you may want to consider allowing him this leeway, as long as the outcome is acceptable.

See the good in people. Everybody's "weird." You are too, to someone. Remember this as you are tempted to judge people. Learn to look at everyone as being full of potential and wanting to contribute. Adopt that attitude in all of your employee interactions. You may be disappointed when you occasionally encounter someone who is more unpleasant than pleasant, or more unable than able, but for the most part you will be giving your employees every opportunity to succeed.

Don't lose sight of yourself. As you try to please others, don't lose sight of yourself. Take time for yourself, and give yourself the same recognition, appreciation, support, and development you would give to your employees. After all, there may be no one else providing these things to you. To maintain your sanity and ability to produce good results, you may have to say, "No," to people sometimes, even to your manager. Don't feel that you have to answer people right away; if you need time to think before making a commitment to someone, ask for it. If you have many obligations and you don't know which ones you are able to refuse, ask your manager for guidance.

Your job is not going to be easy, but it will be easier if you implement *MeYouQ*. Stay mindful about the situations you find yourself in, and how your personal traits might be affecting your actions and reactions. Work to recognize, understand, and manage all of the parts that make up the wonderful person you are. Get to know others, reserve judgment, and appreciate each one as a unique individual. Have the kinds of conversations you need to have in order to build relationships.

Your *MeYouQ* will grow and develop over the course of your life as you work to understand yourself and others better, and encounter different people and new situations. You have the tools, and they will work with most people, though occasionally you may have to admit defeat and terminate a relationship. For people leaders, however, the immediate goal is to develop your *MeYouQ* and put it into action to create a supportive, mentally healthy, and productive department, team, or workplace.

Please visit the website at www.meyouqbook.com
to share your stories and ideas.

Acknowledgements

Thank you for aspiring to be a better leader for the people in your life, for sharing my passion of wanting people, all people, to be treated better in the workplace, and for purchasing this book to help get you started. Congratulations on choosing to make good mental health a priority in your life; this is a decision I know you won't regret. I hope you will truly embrace the *MeYouQ* concept, so you can understand yourself better and experience enhanced, positive relationships with the people in all areas of your life.

To my husband, Paul, you are the best partner I could hope for in this life. With you, I feel a sense of freedom from negativity and drama; it's just fun and easy, even when we are working hard. Your support and acceptance have provided me with the fuel I need to live my best life. I love you and our evolving future together. Who knows what we will be doing next!

To my daughters, Alexa and Dani Chobotar, my wish for each of you is a lifetime of joy and success in whatever you choose to do. My *MeYouQ* journey began when you were little, and I could see that each of you was a unique individual with a variety of traits that required me to relate to you a certain way. Alexa, you know what you like and what you want in this world. This will give you the focused passion to achieve your goals and be admired in the things you do. Dani, you have a vision for how things should be and are not afraid to stand up for what you believe in. You are going to change things for the better wherever you go. I am very proud of you both and look forward to your amazing futures.

To my mom, Stella Larson, I want to thank you for being strong in your life, so I could grow in the ways I needed to. You are still a very important part of my life, and I continue to appreciate you being there.

To my editors, Craig Dyer and Shauna Stevenson, my very good friends, thank you for giving me honest feedback, and for your time and attention to the manuscript. Craig, you have always been a mentor and cheerleader in my professional life. Your positive feedback has meant so much to me and my development over the years. Shauna, your love for and kindness towards others is inspiring. You have been an important confidante in my life and have given me a sense of home as the big sister I never had. You have both added so much to this manuscript!

Thank you to Susy, Jim, and everyone else who has impacted my life, both personally and professionally, there are too many to mention everyone's individual contribution. You have each helped me live my purpose!

With love, Treena

Biographies

Author, Treena Chabot has been on a life-long quest to make things better, especially when it comes to improving how bosses treat their employees. She presents knowledge and best practices from her 17+ years' experience in educating and training aspiring business professionals. Her years of experience include developing conflict avoidance methodologies and guiding teams to consensus decisions.

Treena is a Chartered Professional in Human Resources (CPHR) who believes the key to workplace engagement and satisfaction is having supervisors who build positive relationships with all of their employees. She possesses Bachelor of Commerce (Hons.) and Bachelor of Education degrees. Treena owns the company TREE for Supervisors, where she develops supervisors and advises on the Psychological Health and Safety standard.

For leisure, Treena is a sports fan and loves reading. She enjoys live rock and country music and finds serenity in palm trees.

Content Editor, Craig Dyer has over 20 years of experience in private industry in a variety of marketing capacities, as well as serving over 10 years as a college business instructor. Over his years as a marketing instructor, he has enjoyed mentoring students, and being involved in bridging activities between academics and industry via his involvement in various competitions and student work-placement activities.

Craig holds Bachelor of Commerce (Hons.) and Bachelor of Arts degrees as well as a number of executive development courses. He holds a lifetime membership with the Canadian Professional Sales Association.

Outside of his work he has a passion for discovery through world travel and exploration, exercise, and exhilaration through his bicycles.

Copy Editor, Shauna Stevenson has over 10 years of experience in the biotechnology industry and has participated in several publications. Over her career she has worked in research and development, quality assurance and clinical operations support.

Shauna holds Bachelor of Science (Hons.) and Master's of Science (Biochemistry & Medical Genetics) degrees, and is certified as an auditor. She has a passion for helping people achieve success, and works as a Supervisor Development Specialist with TREE for Supervisors to help people build stronger, more productive relationships. She continues to consult in the biotech industry and works occasionally as a copy editor.

Shauna enjoys traveling, outdoor activities, including cycling and hiking, and time at the lake with family and friends.

Please see the copyright page for contact information on the editors. Contact the author at www.meyouqbook.com.

Index

Made in the USA
Columbia, SC
05 May 2018